T0288274

CONCISE
LINCOLN
LIBRARY

—

EDITED BY RICHARD W. ETULAIN,
SARA VAUGHN GABBARD, AND
SYLVIA FRANK RODRIGUE

FERENC MORTON SZASZ
WITH MARGARET CONNELL SZASZ

Lincoln and Religion

Southern Illinois University Press
Carbondale

17 16 15 14   4 3 2 1

The Concise Lincoln Library has been made possible
in part through a generous donation by the Leland E.
and LaRita R. Boren Trust.

Library of Congress Cataloging-in-Publication Data
Szasz, Ferenc Morton, 1940–2010.
Lincoln and religion / Ferenc Morton Szasz, Margaret
Connell Szasz.
    pages   cm. — (Concise Lincoln library)
Includes bibliographical references and index.
ISBN 978-0-8093-3321-9 (hardback)
ISBN 0-8093-3321-X (cloth)
ISBN 978-0-8093-3322-6 (ebook)
    1. Lincoln, Abraham, 1809–1865—Religion. 2. United
States—Religion—19th century. 3. Presidents—Reli-
gious life—United States. I. Szasz, Margaret. II. Title.
E457.2.S97 2014
973.7092—dc23   2013034620

Printed on recycled paper. ♻

The paper used in this publication meets the minimum
requirements of American National Standard for
Information Sciences—Permanence of Paper for
Printed Library Materials, ANSI Z39.48-1992. ♾

CONTENTS

ILLUSTRATIONS

Following page 56

SERIES EDITOR'S PREFACE

Richard W. Etulain

Triumph and tragedy propelled this book. For over forty years, Ferenc Morton Szasz enjoyed a remarkably productive career. A scholarly specialist in American social and cultural history, he produced a number of notable monographs and hundreds of essays and reviews on those subjects. At the University of New Mexico, he was also recognized as a superb teacher, drawing thousands of students to such packed-out courses as The U.S. and World War II, History of Religion in America, and American Social and Intellectual History.

Early on, Szasz exhibited a strong interest in Abraham Lincoln. He overloaded his shelves with numerous books on Lincoln, lectured on Lincoln in his courses, and made numerous presentations on Lincoln, particularly to lay audiences in New Mexico and Great Britain. Szasz's career-long interest reached a new height in the publication of his book *Abraham Lincoln and Robert Burns: Connected Lives and Legends* (2008). The very readable volume provided a thorough comparison of the lives and thoughts of these two notable figures. An especially valuable contribution of the book was the author's careful discussion of the diverse religious experiences of Lincoln and Burns.

More than a decade ago, I invited Szasz to coauthor or coedit a volume on Lincoln and religion. When complications brought overloads to both of our schedules, the idea was shelved—but not forgotten. Later, when I became one of the coeditors of the multi-volume Concise Lincoln Library, I invited Frank Szasz to be the sole author of a brief study of Lincoln and religion. He accepted the invitation but warned me that other projects needed to be finished first. As soon as time allowed, he wanted to work on this project that had interested him for several years.

Then leukemia launched a virulent attack. In February 2010, as Professor Szasz was finishing work on a previous project and commencing the present volume, he was forced out of the classroom and into a hospital room. But he did not give up.

Once begun in earnest, this book sped along. As Szasz had done with his many other books and essays, he composed the manuscript on legal-sized yellow tablet pages. Those early versions were nearly indecipherable—except to a very few who could read Szasz's scribbles. His wife, Margaret Connell Szasz, and two daughters, Chris Garretson Bradley and Maria Szasz, as well as son, Eric Garretson, were members of the chosen tribe who could parse out Frank's scrawl. They have done mighty work in turning Frank's original draft, written under the most trying of physical circumstances, into a readable, revealing, and helpful study of Lincoln and religion.

Had Frank been granted more time, he undoubtedly would have added to his manuscript. He surely would have expanded on Lincoln's increasing interest in things religious in his last years in the White House. Probably he would have done more, too, with Lincoln's connections and correspondence with ministers and rabbis who met or wrote to the president. Other topics would also have been expanded.

Knowledgeable readers will recognize how much Szasz's contentions coincide with conclusions advanced on Lincoln and religion in the past two generations. Szasz avoids the mistaken notion of making Lincoln into a traditional Christian, on the one hand, and of turning him into a cynical atheist, on the other. Rather, he demonstrates that Lincoln gradually found additional consolation in religious experiences. Some of this encouragement came from contacts with two Presbyterian ministers following the deaths of Lincoln's sons Eddie and Willie. Other advancements on his religious journey derived from Lincoln's deep ponderings of the role of God in the horrendous Civil War. Finally, Szasz shows that these steps forward clearly influenced Lincoln's political decisions and policies such as those revealed in the Emancipation Proclamation, the Gettysburg Address, and the Second Inaugural Address.

In this attractively written volume, Frank Szasz provides a needed brief introduction to Abraham Lincoln and religion. It is fitting that Szasz's final volume focuses both on Abraham Lincoln, a man he much admired, and on religion, a centrally important subject to which he devoted so much of his career.

ACKNOWLEDGMENTS
Ferenc Morton Szasz

F irst, I thank my friend and former colleague Richard W. Etulain for inviting me to write this book. I have been teaching a class on the history of religion in America for over twenty years at the University of New Mexico and always include a full class meeting on the faith of Lincoln. This opportunity to expand that lecture into a brief book intrigued me, especially so since the issue of organized religion seems to loom so large in our contemporary world. (It did so in Lincoln's as well; the more things change . . .)

I also thank my family, especially my wife, Margaret, for listening to so many Lincoln stories over the years, as well as my colleagues at the Frontier restaurant lunch table: Rob Robbins, Mel Yazawa, David Holtby, Charlie Steen, and Noel Pugach. Maria Szasz and Chris Garretson Bradley did the word processing, for which I will be eternally grateful.

ACKNOWLEDGMENTS
Margaret Connell Szasz

Ferenc Morton Szasz completed a handwritten initial draft of this manuscript when he was hospitalized in the early spring of 2010. Despite the unrelenting force of his adversary—leukemia—and his extensive chemotherapy treatment, he vowed to complete a draft while he was still able to do so. After he lost that struggle against leukemia in the early summer of that year, our daughter Maria Szasz translated those faint penciled words written on long yellow pads into a typed version, draft number two. Since Ferenc always anticipated writing at least four or five drafts of any book manuscript, we suspected much diligence lay ahead. In response, Charlie Steen, my colleague and history department chair, University of New Mexico, Albuquerque, graciously obtained a course reduction for me so I could make the revisions during the spring term of 2012. The course release proved essential, but so, too, was the crucial support of my family. Relying on a combination of family members—including Maria Szasz, who checked on data and retyped the bibliography; our daughter Chris Garretson Bradley, who chased down further elusive data, helped resolve issues through endless phone conversations, and, once again, took over the formatting of the manuscript; and our son, Eric Garretson, who served as our backup volunteer—I managed to pound out six more drafts during those months. During the summer of 2012, Tyler Bradley also jumped aboard the family effort by searching for illustrations for the manuscript.

Along the way, I relied on a number of other friends, whom I also thank. These include my colleagues Durwood Ball, Cathleen Cahill, Paul Hutton, Pat Risso, Sam Truett, and Andrew Sandoval-Strausz. I also thank my former colleague Richard W. Etulain, who took the time out of his fast-paced schedule to read a full draft and contribute many helpful suggestions. He also wrote a splendid historiographical essay for the manuscript. Further, Alison Brown, colleague at the University of Aberdeen, Scotland, offered inspired ideas during the summer of 2011. The history department staff, which ranks as the best in any department at UNM, has supported me throughout this project, and I am much in debt to Yolanda Martinez, Dana Ellison, Helen Ferguson, and Barbara Wafer.

At Southern Illinois University Press, I appreciate the encouragement of Sylvia Frank Rodriguez, SIU Press executive editor. Given the circumstances, she has made the transition as smooth as possible. Sara Gabbard, one of the editors of SIU Press's Concise Lincoln Library series, provided the excellent section of Lincoln quotes and offered wonderful detailed suggestions for the manuscript revisions.

I also thank the two outside reviewers for SIU Press, whose ideas I have sought to incorporate into the final draft. I remain especially indebted to the first outside reader, whose generous comments spurred my efforts.

Completing this manuscript in a manner that would retain the core of Ferenc's research and the many decades he spent pondering the complexities of Abraham Lincoln has been my goal. En route, I have become almost as enamored of our sixteenth president as Ferenc was, though I shall never achieve the depth of understanding or breadth of knowledge that he gained through his study of Lincoln and the earlier works that he published on the president. Ferenc connected with Lincoln, shared many of his beliefs, found a kindred spirit in his humor, and was humbled by his greatness. I am now grateful to understand a little of that attachment for a man whose compassion for humankind has left an indelible legacy for all generations of Americans and whose greatness has been recognized around the earth.

LINCOLN AND RELIGION

OPENING: LINCOLN'S
FAITH PERSPECTIVE

In the bicentennial year of Abraham Lincoln's birth, 2009, historian Michael Burlingame penned a two-volume, 1,976-page biography titled *Lincoln: A Life*. This work can only be described as "magisterial." Toward the end of volume 2, the author came up with a trenchant observation: "Lincoln's personality was the North's secret weapon in the Civil War, the key variable that settled the difference between victory and defeat."

This brief book will push Burlingame's step a little further along the historical chessboard. I plan to argue that one key to Lincoln's personality—especially during the presidential years—rested with his evolving faith perspective. And for this interpretation of Lincoln's faith, I borrow, for the moment, the words of twentieth-century theologian Paul Tillich, who described faith perspective as an area of "ultimate concern." With Lincoln, one should use the phrase "ultimate concern" in the plural, for the president's faith revolved around two ideological systems that overlapped in ways impossible to separate.

As Lincoln observed during the address he delivered in Philadelphia's Independence Hall on February 22, 1861, his personal political views, confirming his Whig perspective, stemmed directly from Thomas Jefferson's Declaration of Independence: "It was something in the Declaration of Independence giving liberty not only to the people of this country, but hope to the world for all coming time. It was that which gave promise that in due time the weights should be lifted from the shoulders of all men, and that *all* should have an equal chance." In Lincoln's view, the American Republic was the best system of government ever created, and as a Whig admirer of Henry Clay, he acknowledged the significance of personal responsibility and morality and individual striving among the people who lived in this Republic. Under the American system of laws, the minority held rights that had to be respected, but ultimately the will of the majority must prevail. The only alternative, Lincoln believed, was anarchy.

And even in his search for a "faith perspective," Lincoln grappled with traditional views of Jesus Christ that had emerged among the common people who settled in the Ohio Valley during his youth. Like so many of his generation, Lincoln read deeply in the King James Version of scripture—the book through which he tried to comprehend the mysterious working out of God's plans for humankind. For Lincoln, God worked within the confines of history to enact his will.

These cosmic neologistic systems, for surely they were so, contained a built-in tension. As historian Sydney E. Mead has noted, the religion of the Republic often contained an "inclusive" system, in theory at least, that was open to all. On the other hand, biblical Christianity in an American context had long been altered from its antecedents. From the colonial era forward, American Christianity was drawn into denominationalism, which introduced an exclusive dimension, thus placing a permanent tension at the heart of the American experimentation in self-government. But, it must be emphasized at the onset: as far as Lincoln was concerned, his own faith was not frozen in time.

The outstanding feature of Lincoln's life was his capacity for development. Neither a born genius nor a man of mediocre talents suddenly endowed with wisdom to guide the nation through the trials of a civil war, he developed gradually, absorbing from his environment that which was useful and good and growing in character and mind.

The overlapping of these inseparable features is the keynote of Lincoln's "faith perspective." This brief study provides the first direct analysis of Lincoln's religion for a full generation, and it moves the ongoing assessment into the twenty-first century.

People new to the field of Lincoln studies are often astounded at the vehemence of historical disagreement. Historian David Herbert Donald once pointed out that the latest Lincoln interpretations often offered "more of the same." The religion of no other chief executive of the American Republic has called forth such intense historical scrutiny. It is widely known that George Washington was an Episcopalian with one foot in the Deist camp. Woodrow Wilson was a Presbyterian; Herbert Hoover, a Quaker; Franklin Delano Roosevelt, an Episcopalian; John Fitzgerald Kennedy, a Catholic; George H. W. Bush, an Episcopalian; George W. Bush, a conservative evangelical; and Barack Obama, a Congregationalist. Other presidents also fit into well-known faith parameters.

But aside from various partisan campaign squabbles during election time, any concern about other presidents' faiths has long since passed into antiquarianism. Not so for Lincoln. Virtually the entire religious spectrum claims right of possession for this American president. Every faith claims Lincoln as "theirs." Today even American atheists declare Lincoln to be one of their own, as do the Baptists, Presbyterians, Quakers, Episcopalians, Spiritualists, and even the Jews. A contemporary Disciples of Christ tale includes him in their legends. A Church of the Brethren tradition suggests Lincoln had plans to convert to their pietistic faith just before his assassination. The faith of no other American president commands the broad-based attention as the faith of Abraham Lincoln.

The public controversy regarding the specific nature of Lincoln's faith began in 1873, when pastor James Reed suggested in *Scribner's Monthly* that Lincoln was Christian. This public claim brought former law partner William Herndon off his chair, and Herndon spent the rest of his life trying to prove Lincoln was a nonbeliever. The unrelenting argument, begun in the nineteenth century and continuing into the twenty-first, has yet to reach a resolution.

The actual facts of Lincoln's church attendance are fairly well known. As a youth, Lincoln attended regular (or Primitive, also sometimes called Hardshell) Baptist services in Kentucky and Indiana with his family. He may have served the church as sexton for teaching while he was courting Mary Todd in Springfield in the 1840s, and he almost surely attended Protestant Episcopal services with her during their courtship. After their marriage in 1842, the Lincolns continued to attend Episcopal services; in addition, the family eventually purchased a pew at First Presbyterian Church in Springfield. While living in the White House, the Lincoln family attended Dr. Phineas D. Gurley's Second Presbyterian Church (also known as New York Avenue Presbyterian Church) in Washington, D.C.; a plaque located within the church marks the pew where they sat.

When he ran for Congress against widely known Methodist minister Peter Cartwright in 1846, most of Springfield's churches opposed Lincoln as an "infidel," a charge that hurt him considerably. He planned to issue a statement that year regarding his faith, denying he was in that camp. But when he ran for reelection as U.S. president in 1864, although the faith issue resounded in American denominations, the majority of the evangelical churches gave him their support. This endorsement pleased him very much; he let this evangelical backing confirm his official statement that he was not an "infidel."

In spite of his periodic attendance at formal services, Lincoln retained a strong skeptical streak throughout his lifetime. Further, he remained aloof from denominational claims. As he once phrased it, "When any church will inscribe over its altar as its sole qualification for membership the Savior's condensed sentiment as the substance of both law and gospel, 'Thou shalt love God with all thy heart, all thy soul, and all thy mind, and thy neighbor as thyself,' that church I join with all my heart and soul."

Thus, Lincoln's road to comprehending the role of Providence in the destiny of human affairs lay less with the various Protestant denominations than in the King James Version of scripture itself. Limited by the number of books available during his youth, yet gifted with an incredible memory, the young Lincoln memorized long passages from both the Old and New Testaments.

Any historical analysis of Lincoln's faith must begin with a number of caveats. First, Lincoln remained vigorous in his support for

Christian ethics, but he was silent regarding his personal religious perspective. In the absence of his own words, scholars have had to rely frequently on the statements of others, many of whose comments, as David Donald has observed, are especially unsubstantiated. Second, researchers would do well to place his various theological statements within their appropriate context because every one of Lincoln's theological observations proved amply rested in the theories of his pre-Darwinian era.

In short, while scholars may attempt to assess Lincoln's evolving religious faith, in reality, one can never assume, with perfect certainty, where he stood. That simply is not possible. All scholars can do is approximate the case with the best care, seeking to understand this dimension of the president within Lincoln's well-anchored faith in the Republic and the biblical wisdom he had absorbed from his youth forward. Lincoln's memories of his youth have continued to haunt scholars even after he discerned the will of Providence in himself and long after he became the center of the nation's "civil religion."

THE OHIO RIVER VALLEY:
KENTUCKY, INDIANA, AND ILLINOIS

Although the historical faith of the Lincoln family began in the East Anglia county of Norfolk, where they were Congregationalists, and later shifted to the faith of the Quakers when they migrated through New Jersey and Pennsylvania in the mid-eighteenth century, by the time they had reached Kentucky by way of Virginia's Shenandoah Valley, they were firmly ensconced within the Baptist camp. Since young Abraham was only eight years old when his father, Thomas, moved the family across the Ohio River in 1816, Lincoln could not have had much meaningful contact with church circles until then. While they were living in Indiana, Lincoln's older cousin Dennis Hanks and Lincoln's sister joined the teenage section of the Little Pigeon Creek Baptist Church in Spencer County. Members of the Pigeon Creek church congregation were Calvinist, but they were also Separatist Baptists who held an anti-mission stance that emerged from their extreme position on Calvinism.

Few of the Ohio River Valley sermons of that era have survived, but scholars can make some educated guesses regarding both their content and quality. Saint Augustine once argued that there were three parts to an effective sermon: tell a story, provide theological instruction, and set forth an ethical challenge to the listener for future behavior. Since the Baptists and Methodists had established few formal requirements for preachers in Lincoln's day, they were seldom able to achieve this goal. The grandson of Baptist minister

David Elkin, who presided over the grave of Nancy Lincoln, allegedly knew but a single letter of the alphabet—the letter *O* because it
was round. Yet young Lincoln gained a local reputation for listening
to sermons and parodying them, speaking from a stump platform
much to the delight of his listeners. But to completely ridicule these
frontier clergy for their garbled gospel interpretations is also to slight
the pervasive oral tradition that reigned in the Ohio River Valley
during Lincoln's youth.

From the 1790s to roughly the 1830s, the theology of America's
common people emerged. Standing squarely on scripture, men and
women became their own theologians. Not only were they convinced
they had heard God's Word, they also felt compelled to explain it to
others. The theologies of the people had staked a claim in the young
nation. Newly minted preachers could neither read nor write, but
their dwelling on God's plan to free the children of Israel from Egypt
held rapt attention. The Bible, they maintained, never speaks of
"rights"; instead, life is always a gift. Sermons on the transcendence
of God, the importance of forgiveness, and the need to temper justice
with mercy could all have important application, extreme though
the presentation might have been. In addition, especially in interior
regions like the Ohio Valley, a sermon served as a form of entertain-
ment and a constant source of conversation afterward, both of which
were essential components in a decidedly hardscrabble world.

The type of minister encountered by Lincoln in early nineteenth-
century America remained an essential part of America's southern
culture for three generations. He makes an appearance in the life of
Mark Twain's Huck Finn, who describes former preacher Silas Phelps
in the following words: "He was the innocent, best old soul I ever
see. But it wasn't surprising: because he wasn't only just a farmer, he
was a preacher too, and had a little one-horse log church down back
of the plantation, which he built it himself at his own expense, for a
church and a schoolhouse and never charge nothing for his preaching
and it was worth it too. There was plenty other farmer-preachers like
that, and done the same way, down south."

But religion for Lincoln transcended mere preaching. For him,
religion enlarged upon themes of ethics and compassion. When I do

good, I feel good, he once said; when I do bad, I feel bad. In addition, Lincoln also embraced an enormous amount of compassion. He hated to shoot wild game and once remarked that an ant's hope is as sweet to the insect as ours is to us. Contemporary theologian Karen Armstrong once said: "Compassion does not mean 'pity.' It means 'to experience with' the other. The golden rule of always treating another as you would wish to be treated yourself lies at the heart of all morality. It requires a principled, ethical and imaginative effort to put self-interest aside and stand in somebody else's shoes." And for Lincoln's antebellum world, the overarching theme of compassion formed an integral dimension of the issue of chattel slavery.

Slavery and Ethics

For Lincoln, taking a stand on slavery would become integral to his growth as a compassionate human being. But Lincoln also had a practical side, and this aspect of his character could be seen in the early years of his involvement with the South's "peculiar institution," tentacles of which reached up into Illinois. During her childhood in Kentucky, Mary Todd had grown up with slaves. Yet Lincoln, from his youth, expressed these feelings, "If slavery is not wrong, nothing is wrong." The fact that he had to turn over all his wages to his father until he reached the age of twenty-one, combined with the persistent poverty of his youth, gave him a direct acquaintance with the institution. "I have seen a good deal of the backside of the world," he once remarked to an Illinois neighbor.

Still, Lincoln's pragmatism on this issue persisted. On March 3, 1837, Lincoln and a co-legislator presented a statement in the Illinois legislature, a "protest" against a recently passed set of pro-slavery resolutions. The protest declared "that the institution of slavery is founded on both injustice and bad policy, but that the promulgation of abolition doctrines tends rather to increase than abate its evils." The last reference regarded the case of abolitionist Elijah P. Lovejoy, also known as X., of Alton, Illinois, whose assassination reinforced the power of slavery in southern Illinois.

As a member of Congress during the Mexican-American War, Lincoln attempted to create a bill to abolish slavery in the District of Columbia, but it was never introduced. Still, in 1847 he had long proved his view of slavery when he said, regarding the slavery question, "God will settle it and settle it right, and . . . He will, in some inscrutable way, restrict the spread of so great an evil."

By the mid-1850s, Lincoln had begun to find his voice on this issue, and the passage of the Kansas-Nebraska Act in 1854 led him to take a passionate stance. Stephen A. Douglas's act declared the Missouri Compromise null and void and granted citizens of the new territory of Kansas the right to introduce slavery into the territory. The southern border of Missouri no longer marked the northern boundary of slavery, and the act meant slavery expansion was now a distinct option. Further, Douglas's shrewd solution—popular sovereignty or territorial option—offered a slippery angle to both North and South. As an intensified focus on the issue of slavery versus "free soil" in the territories entered the center stage of American politics, it also spurred the creation of the Republican Party. The Kansas-Nebraska Act was pivotal for the nation and for Abraham Lincoln.

In the famous Lincoln-Douglas debates of 1858, Lincoln nailed Douglas at the second debate, held in Freeport, Illinois, where Douglas defended the rights of territorial citizens to exclude slavery. In his argument, which was quickly dubbed the Freeport Doctrine, Douglas struggled to rescue the viability of popular sovereignty without engaging a moral position. But a morally neutral stance was anathema to Lincoln. To have a moral compass, Lincoln observed, people had to want what was right. Two years later, in his even more elegant Cooper Union speech of 1860, Lincoln argued that the Founding Fathers had hoped to contain the peculiar institution; they had marked slavery "as an evil not to be extended" and had voted to retain the power of the federal government to control slavery in the territories. Indeed, the Founding Fathers themselves had expressed some form of opposition to the expansion of slavery.

The Ohio River Valley

When Abraham Lincoln was born on February 12, 1809, near Hodgenville, Kentucky, his Ohio River Valley frontier world contained precious few luxuries. His father, Thomas, erected log cabins twice in

Kentucky, again when he moved the family to Indiana in 1817, and yet again in Illinois in 1830. Thomas dabbled in carpentry, hunted, and farmed, planting potatoes, corn, and various vegetables, all of which barely kept the wolf from the door. Borrowing the words of Thomas Gray, Lincoln would describe his early life as "the short and simple annals of the poor."

But if his early Ohio River Valley world lacked material goods, it also overflowed with promise. Two systems of belief spoke directly to the potential of the average citizen: the ancient biblical account of human destiny as found in the scriptures and the eighteenth-century Enlightenment promises of an egalitarian republican government, as embodied in the Declaration of Independence, the Constitution, and the ongoing acts of the president, the Supreme Court, and Congress.

These worldviews did not flow in separate tracks; rather, they overlapped in myriad ways. For many of Lincoln's generation, the words of scripture and the words of the Declaration and the Constitution both embodied God's plan for the American nation. Equally important, both traditions came to focus on that most powerful of all social forces—the potential destiny (in religious terms, salvation) of the ordinary person.

Lincoln grew to maturity surrounded by these overlapping sacred symbol systems, and he internalized them in his own unique fashion. The Enlightenment faith in reason as the sole guide to life and the biblical account of God working out his mysterious ways through human actions within the confines of time and history—in varying proportions—would ever remain part of his world.

Religious Background

The religious world surrounding Abraham Lincoln's youth remained in perpetual turmoil. After the close of the Revolution, a variety of Deist tracts found readership on the frontier. In Kentucky, the legislature actually dismissed its chaplain as superfluous. The two most powerful churches of colonial America, the Congregationalists of New England and the Church of England, which was most prominent in the South, found it difficult to cross the Appalachian Mountains when the young Republic came into being. Only a loose alliance with the

Presbyterians—with whom they were very close theologically—allowed the Congregationalists to spread west from New England to the northern sections of Ohio, Indiana, Illinois, and Iowa. The Church of England—reconstituted as the Protestant Episcopal Church—faced similar difficulties. Although Episcopalians were usually able to garner support from the local town and country elite, their numbers never grew rapidly in the expanding nation. Historian David L. Holmes has even termed them "an ecclesiastical exotic" in antebellum America.

In lieu of the colonial stalwarts, the churches that dominated the Ohio River Valley consisted of varieties of Baptists, Methodists, and Presbyterians; the Disciples of Christ sprang up later. Rejecting the need for reasoned theological training, Baptists and Methodists accepted as clergy those who felt called to serve. Each church polity also fit well with the demands of the Ohio River Valley frontier. A handful of people could create an independent Baptist church, and an itinerant Methodist circuit rider could cover on horseback a vast area in need of his preaching services. Many—but not all—Baptists held a modified Calvinist interpretation that God had chosen those to whom he would offer His grace before time began. But the Methodists emphasized the Arminian position: every person possessed free will and could extend his or her hand to receive God's freely offered salvation. And the ever-present revival meeting emerged as the major institution by which these ideas reached the citizens who had moved into this frontier region.

These denominations filled an authentic social need. By the 1840s, virtually every Ohio River Valley community boasted at least one Baptist church. The Methodists were everywhere. At one time, there were almost as many Methodist churches in America as post offices. To celebrate their success, the Methodists composed a ditty:

> The world, the Devil and Tom Paine
> Have tried their best, but all in vain
> They can't prevail; the reason is
> The Lord prefers the Methodist.

In addition to these mainstream denominations, Lincoln's youth abounded with nearby semi-utopian social experiments. The Shaker community in Pleasant Hill, Kentucky, lay only about 70 miles from Hodgenville. Robert Owen's New Harmony, Indiana, was situated about 60 miles west of Lincoln's home in southern Indiana. And the Church of Jesus Christ of Latter-day Saints established Nauvoo, Illinois, about 130 miles northwest of Springfield, in the late 1830s and early 1840s. It is virtually certain that conflicting views of these colonies and utopian experiments found their way into the Lincoln family household discussions, for then, as well as now, religion formed an integral and ever-fascinating aspect of the human condition.

Thomas and Nancy Lincoln were members of a Baptist church in Kentucky. When they moved to Indiana in 1817, they joined the Little Pigeon Creek Baptist Church. This was a Regular Baptist church of the era, which, in the words of historian William E. Barton, "out-Calvinized Calvin." After Nancy's death, Thomas married the widow Sarah Bush Johnston, and when she merged her three children with Thomas Lincoln's, she joined the Indiana church by letter.

Young Abraham probably witnessed several baptisms in nearby Little Pigeon Creek. Legend has it that he served as church sexton, and surely he contributed his efforts to church work since both his parents were very active in it. There is also testimony that young Lincoln could hear a local sermon and repeat it—with much exaggeration—to the delight of his listeners. This youthful experience is undoubtedly the origin of his famous phrase, regarding ministers, "When I see a man preach I like to think he is fighting bees."

The sermons that Lincoln heard as a young man would have been based on a biblical text and an elaborate/practical application of it. Although we cannot know for certain, it seems unlikely that the sermons contained much intellectual content. As renowned Presbyterian preacher Charles G. Finney recalled in his memoirs about his youth in Oneida County, New York, in the early years of the century: "I recollect very well that the ignorance of the preachers that I heard was such that the people would return from meeting and spend a considerable time with irrepressible laughter at the strange mistakes which had been made and the absurdities which had been advanced." Famed Methodist preacher Peter Cartwright agreed: "Our pocket Bible, Hymn Book and Discipline constituted our library. It is true we could not, many of us, conjugate a verb or parse a sentence, and murdered the King's English almost every lick. But there was a Divine Unction attended the word preached, and those words fell under the mighty power of God, and thus the Methodist Episcopal Church was planted firmly in this wilderness, and many glorious signs have followed and will follow to the end of time."

No minister of the day "prepared" his sermon. Even the highly successful Finney, who was initially trained in the law and later headed Oberlin College in Ohio, simply let the occasion, the Spirit, and the chosen text open up the subject. Thus, it is extremely doubtful if Lincoln heard an educated cleric deliver a well-argued sermon until he moved to Springfield in 1837.

Although these sermons might have been basic, historian William E. Barton defends them as precisely meeting the needs of an eminently basic social world: "A religion less gentle or more refined would not have served so well the rude conditions of the frontier." Historian John Boles agrees: "More liberal Protestant movements never really had a chance in the region [antebellum Kentucky] after the plain folk had tasted the moral fulfillment of rustic revivalism in which individuals were prepared to seize their salvation." It was, he suggests, a genuine folk movement. And it was Abraham Lincoln's childhood world.

The King James Version and Nineteenth-Century America

Historians generally agree that the King James Version of scripture emerged as *the* most familiar book of nineteenth-century America. Americans had a closer acquaintance with it than with any other volume. Noah Webster, famed compiler of the first American dictionary, once observed that the Bible had a major influence "in forming and preserving our national language." Over time, numerous biblical phrases worked their way into common parlance: man does not live by bread alone; at their wits' end; pearls before swine; pride goeth before a fall; a thorn in the flesh; go the second mile; the love of money is the root of all evil; salt of the earth; turn the other cheek; no one can serve two masters; a house divided against itself cannot stand. All of these pithy expressions punctuated everyday conversation during the era of Lincoln's youth.

Although it was a product of a committee of learned scholars, the language of the King James Version conveyed a level of elegance matched only in Lincoln's day by Shakespeare and Robert Burns, the beloved poet of Scotland. As historian Adam Nicolson has noted, the KJV embraced a dignity while it also retained an ambiguity, "a deliberate carrying of multiple meanings beneath the surface of a single text." This "layering" of meanings has given a linguistic heft to the KJV that few subsequent translations could approximate.

Further, as the introduction to the KJV states, this Bible was "intended to be read aloud in churches." The KJV was to be *heard* rather than read in silence. Such was its power that it inspired what T. S. Eliot later termed "the auditory imagination," that is, "the feeling for syllable and rhythm, penetrating far below the conscious levels of thought and feeling, invigorating every word."

Both the words and sounds, of course, wrapped themselves around the myriad stories and texts that served as metaphors of understanding for over two millennia of human experience: the Ten Commandments; the Exodus; the battle of Jericho; the Promised Land; God's covenant with Israel and, by extension, with the Christian church; the Good Samaritan; Jesus's ability to heal the sick; the Sermon on the Mount; the Passion; the Crucifixion; the Resurrection; the ascension into heaven; the continual promise of God's grace to those who keep his commandments. The list could be extended indefinitely.

Although the biblical stories included both rich and poor, they especially resonated with those who were out of power. As critic Erich Auerbach observes in *Mimesis: The Representation of Reality in Western Literature* (1946), the Hebrew Bible expresses a very different view of reality than does its near-contemporary Greek classics by Homer, the *Iliad* and the *Odyssey*. In the Greek works, the focus ever rests with the social elites: Agamemnon, Helen, Hector, Achilles, Odysseus, and Penelope. The poor serve as foils for the aristocracy, as when the old nurse Eurycleia is bathing the long-absent Odysseus and discovers, just above the knee, the scar he sustained through a childhood injury. But in the Hebrew Bible, everyone—rich or poor, Dives or Lazarus, aristocrat or commoner—falls under the dominion of Jehovah. The

New Testament extends this theme to the entire world. The KJV, then, spoke directly to the idea of equality: every person had been made in the image of God.

The KJV appealed to those Americans living on the frontier, such as the Lincolns, but among all the groups who seized on this theme, none grasped it more tightly than the African American slaves. Indeed, the slaves merged the figures of Moses and Jesus into a single savior. Stories of the Exodus became a standard theme in slave sermons and slave songs. Although the biblical stories included both rich and poor, they had a special meaning for those who inhabited the lower rung of society.

Lincoln and the Bible

From his youth, Abraham Lincoln found that he possessed a remarkable memory. Although he never read rapidly, what he had read remained with him. And, of course, from an early age, he read in the KJV, often the only book available in the Ohio Valley. Historian Philip L. Ostergard has combed through Lincoln's *Collected Works* to compile a list of specific KJV quotations, ranging from Genesis (seven) through Proverbs (five) through the Gospels (twenty-eight). All told, Ostergard counted sixty-nine direct biblical references in Lincoln's writings. If one adds the numerous recollections by others on how often Lincoln used scripture to prove a point, the figure would likely double.

These references ranged from the facetious to the solemn. During the Lincoln-Douglas debates, he handed his overcoat to a bystander and said, "Here, you hold my clothes while I 'stone Stephen.'" In Washington, an angry visitor once berated him, but Lincoln stopped him with "Accuse not a servant unto his master lest he curse thee and thou be found guilty." "There is no such passage in the Bible," the visitor retorted, but Lincoln found it in Proverbs the next morning. And he loved to repeat the story of the traveling preacher who asked permission of Thomas Campbell, secretary of state for Illinois, to deliver a series of lectures in the hall of the House of Representatives in the Old State House on "the second coming of our Lord." Lincoln quoted Campbell's reply, "It's no use. If you will take my advice you will not waste your time in this city. It is my private opinion that if the Lord has been in Springfield once, he will not come a second time."

According to reporter Noah Brooks, who knew the president well, Lincoln had memorized most of Isaiah, many of the Psalms (which he deeply admired), scores of Proverbs, and numerous passages from the New Testament, especially the most famous sayings of Jesus. Historian William E. Barton once counted twenty-two biblical references in twenty-five speeches, eight from the Old Testament and fourteen from the New. Lincoln's famous "lost speech" at Bloomington, Illinois, supposedly included six more biblical quotations.

But Lincoln did not stand alone in his familiarity with scriptural passages. As Henry Otis Dwight once declared, the KJV became "the book of the new world." Historian Perry Miller has observed that since antebellum Americans generally understood the world as being about six thousand years old, the tongue of Moses, Joshua, Joseph, and Paul was as familiar to them as recent voices of less than one hundred years earlier.

The words from the Old Testament provided more than their share of metaphors for nineteenth-century political conundrums. Quaker poet John Greenleaf Whittier once termed Daniel Webster an "Ichabod" for his rigorous support of the Compromise of 1850. This reference to Ichabod is likely completely lost on modern readers, but it once was common parlance. Ichabod was the son of Phinehas, born on the day that the Philistines captured the ark of the covenant. The grief of losing Phinehas and his father, Eli, as well as the ark's loss caused Ichabod's unnamed mother to go into labor; she died shortly after giving birth. The book of 1 Samuel states: "And she named the child Ichabod, saying, The glory is departed from Israel: because the ark of God was taken, and because of her father in law and her husband" (4:21). Ichabod's name symbolizes the glory departing from Israel. Abraham Lincoln's famous "House Divided" image was drawn from the Bible, Mark 3:25. In addition, the Old Testament provided literary inspiration for one of America's greatest novels, *Moby Dick*. Herman Melville's most notorious character was "Ahab," and *Moby Dick* opens with "call me Ishmael."

Although Lincoln's stepmother, Sarah Bush Johnston, later remarked that he probably did not read the scriptures as much as he should, his wonderful gift of recall allowed him to commit extensive passages to memory. Unlike many other religious skeptics, Lincoln knew the Bible well.

But Lincoln drew on scripture and preachers' stories in purely secular terms. Just as he could quote scripture without a hint of unctuousness, he often relied on numerous "preacher stories" to make his points with a similar matter-of-fact attitude. For example, a Methodist once complained that a member of the Universalist ministry promised that all would be saved. "But my dear brother," said the Methodist, "let us hope for better things." Use of stories embraced a faith that was deeper than mere facts, and Lincoln's reliance on them may have been grounded in more than an astute memory. In sum, his stories may have expressed his beliefs.

Without this thorough grounding in the lines of scripture, Lincoln could never have delivered his major state papers, the Gettysburg Address, or the Second Inaugural Address. Although these addresses bear the scriptural imprint retained in his memory, the skepticism borne from his youth shines through as well.

The young Lincoln showed an authentic love of words, and as an Indiana teenager, he actually toyed with the idea of being a writer. His relative Dennis Hanks once recalled that Lincoln's initial reading of Robert Burns's verse probably inaugurated his dream of being a poet. Lincoln penned his share of youthful doggerel, including a crude burlesque of a Gentryville wedding, which contained these comments:

> The woman was not taken
> From Adam's feet we see,
> So he must not abuse her,
> The meaning seems to be.
> The woman was not taken
> From Adam's head, we know,
> To show she must not rule him—
> 'Tis evidently so.

The woman she was taken
From under Adam's arm,
So she must be protected
From injuries and harm.

The satirical lines he composed were long remembered in southern Indiana, where local residents recalled these "scraps better than the Bible, better than [Isaac] Watts['] Hymns." In his mocking commentary on one member of the town's leading family, he included these notable lines: "Besides your ill shape proclaims you an ape, / And that never can answer for me."

While Lincoln's more polished verses, such as "My childhood home I see again," mark a distinct improvement, his literary forte clearly lay elsewhere. There were later rumors that the teenaged Lincoln also wrote an essay on temperance. According to the story, the caliber of the essay so impressed Baptist minister Aaron Farmer that he sent it to an Ohio newspaper for publication. Unfortunately, those rumors have never been substantiated. Still, when Lincoln reached his maturity and moved to New Salem, Illinois, he harbored hopes of eventually breaking into print.

Although the Presbyterians, Methodists, and Baptists may well have "conquered" the frontier for evangelical Christianity, their most determined efforts could never completely eliminate the scattered, yet pervasive, influence of Deism. Charles Finney's memoirs note how often he ran into Deists on the upstate New York frontier. Frequently, he admitted, they were men of real stature in the community. In 1831, the region surrounding New Salem had its share of religious groups—Hardshell Baptists, Cumberland Presbyterians, Methodists, and various forms of "healers." Methodist revivalist Peter Cartwright lived in Pleasant Plains, which was only about ten miles away. Yet when Lincoln arrived in New Salem, he fell into the company of freethinkers and remained in their circle for almost all of his years there, absorbing some well-known Deist writings.

While the Ohio River Valley saw the circulation of various Deist tracts, including the writings of French philosopher Voltaire, the most prominent Deist book seems to have been C. F. Volney's *The Ruins, or*

Meditation on the Revolution of Empires: And the Law of Nature (first published in French in 1791 with an English translation following shortly thereafter). A two-hundred-page ramble through time and space, Volney's *Ruins* melded history, philosophy, and travelogue into a single volume.

Volney's overall message, however, boiled down to several key points: that all religion had evolved from the worship of Nature; that Christianity could best be understood as the allegorical worship of the sun; and that for nations to live in peace with one another, they needed to distinguish between disagreements that could be verified and those that could not. As he observed, "That is to say, all civil effort must be taken away from theological and religious opinions." For Volney, the law of nature reigned supreme; it was "alone sufficient" to serve as the world's Ten Commandments. The reason: nature was universal, just, and eminently reasonable.

Perhaps due to its translation, Volney's *Ruins* never achieved the notoriety of Thomas Paine's two-part *The Age of Reason* (1794–95), which proved more elegant in argument and was much better written. Not only was Paine one of the best prose stylists of the day, his compact *Age of Reason*—subtitled *An Investigation of True and Fabulous Theology*—still ranks as the clearest presentation of the Deist perspective yet written. Even critics acknowledged it as a model of precise and logical argument. Paine condemned all organized faith— "I disbelieve them all"—and concluded, in what would become his most famous phrase, "My mind is my own church."

Paine applied his logical scalpel to scripture with considerable relish. Denouncing revelation as "mere hearsay," he termed the Bible a book of riddles and mysteries. He delighted in pointing out contradictions in the Old and New Testaments. Jesus was the son of God only in the sense that God is the father of all humankind. There is no need for revelation as nature provided all the wisdom that one needed to live a full life. As he put it, "The creation is the Bible of the Deist."

Although these two political theorists attacked religion full bore, they also advocated "the sacred dogma of equality" (Volney). Paine phrased it with more clarity: "I believe in the equality of man," he proclaimed on page 1, "and I believe that religious duties consist in doing justice, loving mercy, and endeavoring to make our fellow creatures happy." Paine's mother belonged to the Church of England, but his father was a Quaker, and Paine singled out his father's church as most closely reflecting the true Deist positions. Lincoln would also express great empathy with the Quakers when they were struggling to remain pacifists in the Civil War.

During the 1830s, Lincoln had a foot in the Deist camp. In the mid-1830s (either 1834 or 1835), while living in New Salem, Lincoln allegedly wrote up a critique of scripture along Deist lines. In several manuscript pages, he pointed to the contradictions of the Bible. Like Paine, Lincoln might well have cited the various statements from the four Gospels—Matthew: "This is Jesus, the king of the Jews"; Mark: "The king of the Jews"; Luke: "This is the king of the Jews"; John: "Jesus of Nazareth, king of the Jews." The assumption, of course, was that such minor discrepancies meant that a person could not trust the narrative. A number of Lincoln's New Salem contemporaries testified to the existence of that "lost manuscript" on Deism.

James H. Matheny, a close friend of Lincoln and a freethinker himself, noted that their group enjoyed talking about religion and that Lincoln would often pick up a Bible, read a passage, and "show its falsity—and its follies on the grounds of *Reason*— . . . finally ridicule it and as it were scoff at it . . . at the fact of contradictions to reason and to itself." Matheny even speculated that Lincoln was an atheist—or close to it.

When Lincoln began showing the much debated manuscript on Deism to his friends, indicating he would be happy to have it published, the alleged tale of his Deism took a different twist. According to an oft-reported story, New Salem storekeeper Samuel Hill realized the damage that such a work could do to an aspiring politician. Concerned, Hill proceeded to grab the manuscript from Lincoln and thrust it into the stove. Other friends shared the same anxiety. William Herndon (who had one foot in the Deist camp but was also the guardian of Lincoln's reputation) lived for years in fear that a fragment of the manuscript or perhaps even a duplicate copy of "the Infidel book" would be discovered. But no such copy or fragment has surfaced, and it is highly unlikely that it ever will.

Manuscript or no manuscript, Lincoln continued to voice his religious skepticism in many forums. He did so even after he moved to Springfield in 1837. But parallel with these attacks on biblical inconsistencies, Lincoln expressed his admiration—in the words of James W. Keyes—"that the System of Christianity was an ingenious one at least—and perhaps was calculated to do good."

The saga of Lincoln's "Infidel book" can best be understood from two perspectives. First, Lincoln may have written this attack in the wake of despair—perhaps even as a direct response to the death in 1835 of Ann Rutledge, who was the first woman Lincoln courted. This intersection between the awesome fact of Rutledge's death and "the thin gruel of humanistic philosophy" drove Lincoln close to the brink of madness, and friends had to watch closely that he did not try to harm himself. So, his "book" may well have been an emotional response to the death of his first romantic love, as he saw her departure as final, without hope of return.

But another interpretation is also possible. In 1834 or 1835, Lincoln had never really written anything of substance, and the so-called Infidel book could not have been more than a brief essay of a few pages. It is quite possible that he actually wrote his essay *before* Ann's death and before he read any Deist writings. Further, none of Herndon's infamous informants could agree on precisely when Lincoln had first read Volney and Paine. A February 15, 1862, article from the *Menard Axis* suggested this position, positing that Lincoln had designed the paper for publication, but his senior friends, pointing him to Paine and Volney (who presented these ideas with more clarity), "brought a change in his intentions, and perhaps his destiny."

Lincoln's Deistic views were well known locally but did not play much of a role until he ran for Congress in 1846 against Methodist cleric Peter Cartwright.

Peter Cartwright

The 1846 congressional race in the Seventh Illinois District pitted Lincoln against famed Methodist circuit-riding parson Peter Cartwright. Like Lincoln, Cartwright was a product of the Kentucky/

Illinois frontier world, and like Lincoln, he was widely known and admired in the Ohio Valley.

Lincoln and Cartwright had crossed paths on a number of occasions. In fact, in Lincoln's first run for the Illinois state legislature in 1832, Cartwright proved one of the successful candidates. Sangamon County merited four representatives, and Cartwright squeaked in at position number four with 815 votes, defeating Lincoln, who came in eighth with 657. This election, Lincoln often observed, was the only time he was ever beaten by a direct vote of the people.

By the 1840s, Cartwright had achieved a near legendary status in Illinois. Born in Virginia in 1785, the young Cartwright and his family soon moved west into Kentucky, selecting an area so far from civilization it was nicknamed "Rogue's Harbor." Converted to Methodism in the great revivals early in the century, Cartwright moved to Sangamon County, Illinois, in 1824, in part to avoid slavery. The Methodist circuit that Cartwright rode covered a gigantic area, from the Kaskaskia River to the northern settlements, including a mission to the Potawatomie Indians. In general, people liked Cartwright. He stood at five-foot-ten, and with his booming voice, he commanded respect. He could out-debate virtually all of his rivals on theology and, when necessary, physically throw them off the church grounds. Lincoln possessed similar talents, and frontier Illinois respected such skills.

During his forty-eight years' residence in Illinois, Peter Cartwright preached more than eighteen thousand sermons and baptized fifteen thousand people into the Methodist church. One historian has commented that his name alone symbolized the western movement of the church during the nineteenth century. He became a legend in his lifetime. In 1856, he published his autobiography, and it remains a classic firsthand account of religion on the frontier.

Still, the overt mixture of religion and politics remained a controversial issue for residents of Illinois. Cartwright served two terms in the state legislature, but in 1835 the Illinois Methodist Conference passed a resolution requesting that its circuit riders leave politics alone. Yet, in 1846, the sixty-year-old Cartwright decided to run one last time against the thirty-five-year-old Lincoln.

In reality, not much separated the Whig Lincoln from the Democrat Cartwright. During the campaign, both spoke in favor of the just-begun Mexican-American War. In a speech in the spring of 1846, Lincoln encouraged volunteering for the war. Both candidates maintained that the evils of slavery could best be ended without abolition, and both favored banking and internal improvements. As Cartwright's biographer Robert Bray has noted, this left only one issue—and the parson seized on it with vigor—Lincoln's lack of any religious affiliation. In the minister's eyes, of course, this stance made Lincoln unfit to represent the Christian citizens of the Seventh District of Illinois.

In truth, it is not clear how much Cartwright actually pushed the theme of Lincoln's apparent lack of Christian faith or infidelity, either in print or on the lecture platform. But surely he must have encouraged the widespread whispering campaign that suggested Lincoln was, at heart, a "Deist."

When he heard those rumors, Lincoln was furious. He issued his first (and only) formal statement on religious matters. Noting that the constitution of Illinois contained no religious qualification to run for office, Lincoln admitted that he was not a formal church member. Still, he insisted that he would never support for office an open scoffer of religion. Moreover, he noted that his belief on the "doctrine of necessity," which he had defended for years, was also a position held by several churches (Presbyterians and Baptists)—a direct slap at Cartwright's Arminian perspective. Those who believed in Arminianism denied predestination; from their perspective, all people will be saved, not just "the Elect."

The most famous exchange along these lines may be found in Carl Sandburg's *Abraham Lincoln: The Prairie Years*. As Sandburg tells it, Lincoln attended a Cartwright service where the minister asked all who wanted to go to heaven to stand, then all who did not wish to go to hell to so do. Everyone stood but Lincoln. "May I inquire of you, Mr. Lincoln, where are you going?" Lincoln's reply: "I am going to Congress."

It is difficult to assess the impact of this accusation of Deism on the election. The Seventh District was solidly Whig; but some

Christian Whigs hesitated to vote for a (probable) infidel. On the other hand, one Democrat so disliked the idea of mixing Methodism and national politics that he promised Lincoln he would cross party lines if Lincoln needed his vote to win. Lincoln asked him to wait until the day of the election, when he sought him out and said he did not really need it: "[I] am now satisfied that I have got the preacher by the [balls], and you had better keep out of the fight." The final vote was not even close: Lincoln won, 6,340 votes to Cartwright's 4,829, a veritable landslide for the 1840s.

Interestingly, Cartwright failed even to mention Lincoln's name in his 1856 autobiography. But the old cleric did end up on Lincoln's side. When Cartwright's grandson was later indicted for murder, and Lincoln, as counsel for the defense, helped get him acquitted, it was much to the old pastor's relief. And Cartwright strongly supported Lincoln's 1860 presidential bid. His later political rhetoric echoed the vehemence of his early theological disputes. Said Cartwright in the *St. Louis Christian Advocate*: "If the Union men need help to kill traitors, call on Illinois. We can send you twenty thousand men, good and true. Rivers of blood will flow, but this Union must stand though the heavens fall."

One later memoir suggests that in 1863, Cartwright at least somewhat regretted his role in the 1846 campaign when he had contributed to the charge that Lincoln was an infidel. He said that some time later he had conversed with Rev. James A. Smith and had gained a much better understanding of Lincoln's quasi-Presbyterian position. Still, as William Herndon noted, although the people of Illinois liked Cartwright personally, the Seventh District did not want to be represented in Washington by a Methodist minister. So, in December 1847, Lincoln took his seat in the Thirtieth Congress.

Mary Todd

All religious history is best placed in cultural context, and Lincoln's religious world moved up a social notch when he began to court Mary Todd during the winter of 1839–40. Born into a prominent family of Lexington, Kentucky, Mary grew up in the Presbyterian church. Yet she also attended Episcopal services, as both served as the denominations of choice for the pioneer planter aristocracy. Dismayed by her father's second marriage, Mary moved to Springfield, Illinois, to live with her sister Elizabeth and brother-in-law Ninian Edwards. Since both of the Edwardses were active Episcopalians, Mary attended the Episcopal church in Springfield for about a decade.

In antebellum America, the Episcopal church, for the most part, did not share in the prevailing evangelical ethos. Relying on the elaborate ritual of the Book of Common Prayer, members of the Episcopal church even viewed the church—not the nation-state—as the primary means of salvation. It was rare for Episcopalians to participate in revivals. Mary was a regular attendee of Episcopal services when Lincoln began courting her, and it is highly probable that he attended these services with her. If so, he surely would have become fascinated with the prayer book, a copy of which lay in every pew. In his inevitable discussions with Rev. Charles Dresser, Springfield's Episcopal priest, Lincoln would have met his first educated cleric. When the couple eventually married in 1842, Reverend Dresser performed the ceremony.

Lincoln's introduction to a second educated cleric of Springfield was the result of a tragic event. On February 1, 1850, after a brief illness, the Lincolns' second son, Eddie, died of pulmonary tuberculosis. Since Reverend Dresser was out of town, Mary asked Rev. James A. Smith, pastor of Springfield's First Presbyterian Church, to deliver Eddie's eulogy. Impressed by his words and manner, Mary began to attend Presbyterian services. The Lincoln family purchased pew 20 (the church held about two hundred members) there and began to attend regularly—she more than he (as was expected by the conventions of the day). They retained the pew until their departure for Washington eleven years later.

Pastor James A. Smith

Born in Scotland, Smith emigrated from his homeland to America as a confirmed freethinker. In 1825, however, he converted in an Indiana camp meeting and joined the Cumberland Presbyterian Church. In a formalized debate with a Mississippi freethinker, Smith wrote a hefty tome, *The Christian's Defense*, published in 1843. During the fall of 1849, Lincoln discovered a copy of Smith's book in the Todd family library in Lexington, and upon the Scot's move to Springfield, Lincoln borrowed a copy from Smith himself. Given the heft of the book, it is unlikely Lincoln ever finished reading it, but he would have approved of Smith's overall approach to religion.

Smith argued that the world ran on a modified Calvinist system, whereby God understood the end of all events even before they had begun. In short, Smith rigorously defended a modified Calvinist system as a layered model, which rested at the core of Lincoln's beliefs. Perhaps one never loses a sense of secularism, but Lincoln's hardcore Deism seemed tempered by his acquaintance with Smith. Smith and Lincoln were both worldly raconteurs, and they enjoyed each other's company. But it was the tragic death of Lincoln and Mary's son Eddie that really brought the two men together.

From Illinois to the White House

After his lone term in Congress (1847–49), Lincoln stepped back from national politics. It was not until 1854, when Stephen Douglas introduced the Kansas-Nebraska Act, with its threat to expand slavery into the territories, that he reentered the national political stage. Discarding his affiliation with the shattered Whig Party, he joined the newly minted Republicans and, in 1856, received a number of votes at the Republican convention to serve as their vice presidential candidate.

In 1858, he accepted the Republican nomination for the Illinois Senate race, responding with his famous "House Divided" speech, and in the late summer and early fall of that year he engaged in the renowned set of debates with Douglas, a contest that would thrust Lincoln into the national spotlight despite Douglas's return to the Senate with the blessing of the Illinois state legislature. Two years later, as the nation was harvesting the bitter legacy of John Brown's raid on Harper's Ferry, the Republican National Convention met, by chance, in Chicago, where astute political maneuvering by Lincoln's supporters engineered his nomination for the presidency on the third ballot. In November 1860, the results confirming Lincoln's victory also promised a national crisis. Within a month, the southern states had begun to secede from the Union.

The election would mark the end of Lincoln's life in Springfield, the home that had witnessed his success in the law and entrance into politics, his marriage to Mary Todd and the birth of their children, and the subtle shift in his faith perspective as he and Mary moved from the Episcopal to the Presbyterian church, where he became acquainted with Pastor Smith.

Smith always felt that his book and subsequent friendship with the Lincolns—he later served as American consul to Dundee, Scotland, during the Civil War—helped bring Lincoln closer to the Reformed faith. This cannot be absolutely proven. But on that rainy day in February 1861, when Lincoln boarded the train in Springfield for his final farewell, he was deeply moved:

> My friends—No one, not in my situation, can appreciate my feeling of sadness at this parting. To this place, and the kindness of these people, I owe every thing. Here I have lived a quarter of a century and have passed from a young to an old man. Here my children have been born, and one is buried. I now leave, not knowing when, or whether ever, I may return, with a task before me greater than that which rested upon Washington. Without the assistance of that Divine Being, who ever attended him, I cannot succeed. With that assistance I cannot fail. Trusting in Him, who can go with me and remain with you and be every where for good, let us confidently hope that all will yet be well. To His care commending you, as I hope in your prayers you will commend me. I bid you an affectionate farewell.

Summary

This chapter has sought to characterize Lincoln's religious perspective up to the moment he spoke these heartfelt words to his Springfield friends on a cold, drizzly February day. He began life as a Hardshell (Calvinist) Baptist, both in Kentucky and Indiana. Thoroughly conversant with chapter and verse of scripture, he developed, on his own terms, a skepticism regarding Christianity. This came to fruition in the "Infidel book" that Samuel Hill thrust into the fire. When he moved to Springfield, where he courted Mary Todd, he advanced several notches in the social hierarchy; he began to move in Episcopal circles, and he probably read the Book of Common Prayer. With the loss of their son Eddie, Lincoln shifted into Springfield's Presbyterian circles. Still, there was little overt religiosity in his makeup until he departed for Washington.

Horace Greeley later noted that when Lincoln boarded the train for the capital, he still remained a man of reason. As his arguments with Douglas and his view of the world suggested, he remained supremely grounded in the sufficiency of reason as an answer for all things. In 1868, Greeley pointed out that Lincoln had maintained great confidence in his ability to influence others. Said Greeley, Lincoln "trained himself to be the foremost *convincer* of his day—the one who could do his cause more good and less harm by a speech than any other living man." Lincoln had convinced his Cooper Union audience in 1860. In 1861, Lincoln still had faith that reasonable statements would do the same for the South, as indicated in the First Inaugural Address. Later on, said Greeley, Lincoln proved he was the "cleverest logician for the masses that providence has yet produced." But in 1861, the South was not about to listen to reason or logic.

LINCOLN AS PRESIDENT: 1861–65

Lincoln made his convoluted journey to Washington in 1861 amid a great deal of confusion. The crowds proved overwhelming, and at times they raged out of control. In New York, for example, he shook two thousand hands and bowed twenty-six hundred times. His short speeches varied, and few contained items of substance. In Lafayette, Indiana, he suggested that the country was bound with "Christianity, civilization and patriotism," for which he was criticized by Cincinnati rabbi Isaac Mayer Wise, who noted that Lincoln received the majority of the non-Christian vote as well. The First Inaugural Address spoke of "intelligence, patriotism, Christianity, and a firm reliance on him who has never yet forsaken the favored land," and a Sabbath observation made in 1865 even used the phrase "the sacred rights of Christian soldiers," among others. Yet Lincoln must have also realized that three-fourths of the white residents of the South were either Baptist or Methodist. Further, he would have been well aware that the entire South—with perhaps more claim to term itself a "Christian civilization"—held a completely opposite view from the stance he had taken on the preservation of the Union. Lincoln rarely repeated that sweeping claim for Christianity and "patriotism" made early in 1861; instead, he couched his inclusive statements in terms of the transcendental nature of the republican experiment. When he stopped in Philadelphia, en route to Washington, for example, he confessed that he had never had a feeling politically that did not flow directly from Thomas Jefferson's Declaration of Independence.

Once ensconced in Washington, Lincoln was abruptly made aware of his role as the target of the American citizen. The new president endured countless hours dealing with office seekers, interspersed with the many people who were more than ready to give him their view of the world. Until his secretaries John G. Nicolay and John Hay restricted the amount of time he devoted to these visits, he spent as much as twelve hours a day in this often tedious task. Since he was frequently displeased with various newspaper editorials, he considered the White House visitors his "bath of public opinion." On one occasion he opened the White House door to an elderly woman who demanded to see Abraham the Second. When asked who the first might be, she said, "Why Lord bless you! We read about the first Abraham in the Bible and Abraham the Second is our President."

Lincoln and the Nation's Faiths

As it turned out, a large number of people were eager to share their views with the president. Interestingly, Lincoln seemed especially annoyed at the various groups of clergymen who invariably brought specific advice for him. When a group of Connecticut clergy called on him in September 1862 and urged him to liberate the slaves, he demurred, noting that while the issue remained ever in his mind, he could not enforce the decree of emancipation, and it would likely resemble the pope's bull against the comet. On one occasion, a man announced that he was the Son of God, but John Nicolay wisely sent him away, urging him to obtain a letter of recommendation from his father.

But Lincoln did not treat all clerical advice with suspicion. When a group of black Baptists from Baltimore presented him with an elaborate copy of the Bible, he spoke in the most generous and gracious terms. On another occasion, a clergyman called on him, and when Lincoln asked what he wished, the man said, "Oh, bless you Sir, I have nothing to say. I merely called to pay my respects." Lincoln rose and shook his hands with vigor: "My dear Sir. I am glad to see you. I am very glad to see you indeed. I thought you came to preach to me."

An important aspect of the church-state encounter during Lincoln's presidency involved the sensitive issue of religious patronage, a subject that has often been overlooked. Overall, Lincoln was highly critical of the caliber of those in the U.S. Army Chaplain Corps, many of whom he considered worthless hangers-on. But the group that caused him the most consternation proved to be the northern Methodists. Large in number and ubiquitous—more so than virtually any other denomination—the Methodists viewed themselves as the "representatives of the American people." Moreover, their bishops often took on active political roles. It was Illinois pastor Peter Cartwright who had run successfully for the state legislature twice and whom Lincoln had defeated in 1846 for a seat in Congress. William G. "Parson" Brownlow proved an active Republican politician during Reconstruction, and Father John Dyer is still considered one of the founders of Colorado. Methodist bishop Matthew Simpson, who paved the way through sermons in support of Colorado, proved a consistent lobbyist for his denomination. Lincoln felt dismay at such sectarian lobbying, however, and confessed that he preferred the Episcopalians to the other denominations because they were indifferent to a man's religion and his politics.

But the Methodists were not the only religious group that Lincoln had to deal with. He also had significant interactions with the Jewish community, the Shakers, the Quakers, the Latter-day Saints, the Spiritualists, and Native Americans.

The Jews

In 1861, the United States contained about two hundred thousand Jews, who were scattered throughout the entire nation. There was no single "Jewish opinion" on slavery, as the Jewish views on the South's "peculiar institution" and secession were largely determined by whether they lived north or south of the Mason-Dixon Line. (It is estimated that about seventeen thousand to twenty thousand Jews owned slaves and that some Jews worked as slave traders.) But geography did not determine everything. Rabbi Morris J. Raphall of New York published a pamphlet, *The Bible View of Slavery*, which defended the institution on biblical grounds.

During the Civil War, the only Jewish cabinet member on either side was Judah P. Benjamin, who served variously as secretary of the treasury, attorney general, secretary of war, and secretary of state for the Confederacy. In Congress, Ohio abolitionist Benjamin F. Wade once scorned Judah Benjamin as an "Israelite with Egyptian principles." After the Union victory in 1865, the controversial Benjamin fled to England, never to return.

One of Lincoln's first dealings with the northern Jewish community was the appointment of a Jewish chaplain in 1861–62, but his second dealing with them proved far more significant. A contentious affair, it involved the overturning of Major General Ulysses S. Grant's infamous General Order No. 11, which provided for the expulsion of the Jews, as a group, from the Memphis region. The order went out from Grant's headquarters, and it affected the entire area under Grant's command. Based in La Grange, Tennessee, Grant had become increasingly furious with the wave of speculators who had descended on the Memphis area to speculate in captured or contraband cotton bales. Although denying that he wished to hamper any honest business enterprise, Grant labeled the speculators thieves and traitors. Many were German Jews.

Thus, on December 17, 1862, Grant issued General Order No. 11, which became known as "the most sweeping anti-Jewish legislation" in American history. General Order No. 11 stated: "The Jews, as a class, violating every regulation of trade tabulated by the Treasury Department, and also Department orders are hereby expelled from the Department within twenty-four hours from the receipt of this order."

Following this order, a storm of protest emerged, led by the large German Jewish community in the Cincinnati region. A delegation arrived in Washington, D.C., on January 3, 1863, accompanied by Representative John A. Gurley of Ohio, and its members stated their case to Lincoln. According to one of the Jews who had been expelled, Cesar Kaskel of Paducah, Kentucky, the exchange went as follows:

"And so the children of Israel were driven from the happy land of Canaan?"

"Yes," replied Kaskel, "and that is why we have come unto Father Abraham's bosom, asking protection."

"And this protection they shall have at once," said Lincoln.

Then, seating himself at the table, he revoked Grant's order. Shortly afterward, Isaac Mayer Wise, the most prominent rabbi of Cincinnati, visited the White House to express his thanks. Assuring Rabbi Wise that he felt no prejudice against any group, especially the Israelites, Lincoln said, "I don't like to see a class or nationality condemned on account of a few sinners."

Further large-scale Jewish involvement with Lincoln came with his assassination. Lincoln was shot on the evening of Good Friday (the beginning of the Jewish Sabbath), and in the year 1865, it also happened to be the fourth evening of Passover. Lincoln breathed his last on Saturday morning, which, as historian Michael Mehlman has noted, presented the rabbis with a terrible dilemma. Should they celebrate the escape from Egypt—a time of great joy—or should they discuss the tragic news of the day? Most chose the latter. Thus, the first public pulpit statements of national grief came from the nation's northern rabbis, rather than from its ministers, a breakthrough that reflects what would eventually be understood as the breadth of the emerging civil religion.

Rabbi Samuel M. Isaacs of Broadway Synagogue in New York City, as well as many of those in his congregation, were frequently in tears during that Saturday service. During morning prayer, they recited the Kaddish or the Hashkabah (a prayer for the dead) for Lincoln. In Philadelphia, Rabbi David Einhorn termed the martyred president a "high-priest of freedom," whose only fault was too much sympathy for the Confederacy. In Baltimore, conservative rabbi Benjamin Szold tried to combine the themes of the day, urging his congregation to find great joy that such a stalwart person had lived among them. All the northern rabbis—whether Orthodox or Liberal, German- or English-speaking—joined in mourning the president that Saturday. Many of them compared him to Moses. It is highly likely that this was the first time that the Kaddish or the Hashkabah was offered in a Jewish house of worship for anyone other than those of the Jewish faith.

The Jewish involvement continued. When Lincoln's body arrived in Chicago, en route to Springfield, Illinois, it lay in the courthouse for two days until a canopy could be erected bearing the Hebrew lament "The brother of Israel is slain upon these high places."

About 125 members of the Jewish community took part in the Washington funeral procession, and over two thousand of the five thousand who marched in the New York procession were of Jewish origin. At a memorial meeting in Union Square, the archbishop of the Roman Catholic Church in New York, a Protestant minister, and a Jewish rabbi all played a role in the funeral service (another forerunner of civil religion). An old family friend of Lincoln's, Julius Hammerslough of Springfield, later served as a link to the Jewish community regarding efforts to raise funds for a proposed monument in Lincoln's honor.

According to the *Cincinnati Commercial* of April 20, 1865, Rabbi Wise said: "Abraham Lincoln believed himself to be bone of our bone and flesh of our flesh. He supposed himself to be of Hebrew parentage, *he said so in my presence*, and indeed he possessed the common features of the Hebrew race, both in countenance and features." (Lincoln's son Robert Todd Lincoln later denied this observation.)

Perhaps the final Jewish accolade came with the allegorical full-length portrait of Lincoln painted by the Charleston-born Jewish artist Solomon Nuñes Carvalho immediately after the assassination. *Abraham Lincoln and Diogenes* currently hangs in the halls of Brandeis University.

Shakers and Quakers

By 1861, there were about five thousand Shakers who regarded Lincoln as a benefactor. One group from South Union in Kentucky petitioned the president for exemption from military service as both Confederate and Union armies had ransacked their resources, stripping them of food, hay, and horses and wagons, burning their fence rails for campfires, and driving them to the edge of poverty. Until the Conscription Act of 1863, Lincoln dealt with each case on an individual basis, and his compassion for these men was well known. Eventually, he solved the conscription question by drafting conscientious objectors and then pardoning them "until called for," which did not occur. Grateful for his intercession, the Shakers sent Lincoln one of their renowned pieces of furniture—a chair—and he wrote a thank-you note acknowledging the gift.

Perhaps because of a long family tradition, Lincoln expressed great sympathy for the Quakers. Both pacifist and abolitionist, the Quaker groups found themselves caught on the horns of an inescapable dilemma after the South fired on the Union-held Fort Sumter, forcing its surrender. Some fought and were disillusioned; others contributed the typical rate of three hundred dollars, not for a substitution but for medical/charity work. Still others served in a noncombatant capacity.

The Quakers visited Lincoln; the most famous of these visits was led by Eliza P. K. Gurney on October 26, 1862. The American widow of a notable British Orthodox Quaker, Mrs. Gurney arrived in Washington with three friends. Upon their meeting with the president, Mrs. Gurney spoke for a few moments; afterward, the small group of Quakers prayed silently in Lincoln's office. Lincoln was deeply impressed. They did not offer specific advice, which Lincoln appreciated. Sometime after their visit, the president asked Mrs. Gurney to write to him. In her August 8, 1863, reply, Mrs. Gurney expressed her "continued hearty sympathy in all thy heavy burthens and responsibilities." She praised the Emancipation Proclamation, and she prayed that "the Almighty . . . may strengthen thee to accomplish *all* the blessed purposes, which . . . I do assuredly believe he did design to make thee instrumental in accomplishing, when he appointed thee thy present post of vast responsibility as the Chief Magistrate." Quaker legend claims that her first letter to the president was discovered in Lincoln's coat pocket after his assassination.

The Latter-day Saints

In late 1861, shortly after the arrival of the telegraph in Salt Lake City, Utah Territory, Brigham Young sent Lincoln a telegram, observing, "Utah has not seceded but is firm for the constitution and laws of our once happy country." Several Saints saw the tragic conflict as a fulfillment of a December 25, 1832, prophecy by Joseph Smith, who observed that the North and South would clash "and then war shall be poured out upon all nations." During the conflict, Brigham Young predicted, the two sides would exhaust themselves, which would allow the Saints to return to the Midwest and establish the true Republic of God. Many Americans thought that the Saints had great respect for the U.S. Constitution, which they believed came directly from the hand of God. Many Saints saw the conflict as divine retribution for their persecution, especially the 1844 mob action in Carthage, Illinois, that had killed the prophet Joseph Smith.

Thus, Lincoln faced a real dilemma. When he learned that Brigham Young was concerned about his election victory in 1860, because it had brought into power a party whose platform promised to eradicate polygamy, Lincoln responded by relating a story to T. B. H. Stenhouse, a Mormon journalist: "Stenhouse, when I was a boy on the farm in Illinois there was a great deal of timber on the farm which we had to clear. Occasionally we would come to a log which . . . was too hard to move, so we ploughed around it. That's what I intend to do with the Mormons. You go back and tell Brigham Young that if he will let me alone I will let him alone."

In April 1862, Lincoln asked Young to provide soldiers to protect the stage (mail) and telegraph line in southern Wyoming, and the Nauvoo Legion did as instructed. In December 1877, the Saints baptized Abraham in proxy.

Native Americans

In 1863, chiefs from the Cheyenne, Arapaho, and Sioux nations traveled to Washington, D.C., to meet with President Lincoln in order to sign special agreements that would make the route of the Santa Fe Railroad safe in exchange for $25,000 per year for five years (gifts were to include goods and presents). But Congress unilaterally rejected this agreement, and when the promised supplies did not arrive, the chiefs were irate. The misunderstandings fostered by this episode, which typified Indian–U.S. government relations, persisted throughout the Civil War. By absorbing the energies of Lincoln, and of many Native people as well, the agonies of America's national conflict led to the diminution of other major concerns, including the Indian policy of Lincoln's presidency. The unending failures of this policy captured Lincoln's attention whenever news of violent confrontations between Indians and white settlers reached the capital. One of the critical events rooted in the nation's disastrous Indian policy exploded in 1862.

The Dakota (Santee Sioux) uprising erupted when Dakota warriors turned to violence against white settlers in protest against their horrendous treatment by the U.S. Indian agents who served as local representatives for the federal government in the newly created Minnesota. Although this uprising could be viewed exclusively as a military conflict, it also highlighted the contrast between the immigrants' Christian faith and the Native religion of the Dakota people, whose faith encompassed a complex, nature-based worldview sustained by ancient ceremonies. Hence, the Dakota uprising was as much a religious clash as a military one, and this cultural dimension of the conflict may have persuaded Lincoln to seek a humanitarian decision in the face of an overwhelming outcry by white Minnesotans, who called for brutal revenge against the Native people.

Following the military defeat of the Dakota people, the U.S. Army, supported by white Minnesotans, fully intended to hang every warrior placed on trial—several hundred men—but the ultimate decision on their fate rested with the president. After being urged by the Episcopal bishop of Minnesota, Benjamin F. Whipple, and many others, Lincoln spared the lives of 264 warriors. The remaining 38 (originally 39; one received a last-minute reprieve) men were hanged. Explaining the careful reasoning that lay behind this decision, Lincoln observed that he was "anxious to not act with so much clemency as to encourage another outbreak on the one hand, nor with so much severity as to inflict real cruelty on the other."

The tragedy in Minnesota, compounded by later disasters, such as the infamous Sand Creek Massacre of Southern Cheyenne and Arapaho people in Colorado, confirmed Bishop Whipple's concerns about the entrenched corruption in the Indian Office. It also heightened Lincoln's awareness of the humanitarian dimension of these issues. Late in 1862, he notified Congress of his fears: "I submit for your especial consideration whether our Indian system shall not be remodeled." Further, Lincoln asked the secretary of the interior to investigate the nation's Indian policy and come up with reform plans. Said Lincoln, if "we get the people through war, and I live, this Indian system shall be reformed."

It is difficult to speculate on a possible postbellum federal approach to Indians under Lincoln's guidance. The Grant Peace Policy, implemented under Lincoln's former general, relied on direction by Christian leaders who, it was assumed, would prove immune to the notorious corruption that had long tainted the Indian Office, as witnessed in the Santee Sioux response. Lincoln's ongoing relationship with the clergy and his humanitarian instincts suggest that, had he lived, he might have pursued a faith-based Indian policy, perhaps with greater success than that pursued by President Grant.

After the war wore thin, Lincoln was exceptionally careful to keep the federal government's hands off all issues of religion and faith. He wisely realized that any meddling had enormous potential for mischief.

In July 1861, the Reformed Presbyterian Church in America sent a missive to its Scottish counterparts. The war had just begun, and church members were dismayed at the possibility of the collapse of the entire nation: "If He pleases to send his judgments and bring down the system of slavery by violent revolution, we submit to His blessed will. If He uses the persuasion of the Gospel for this purpose, we will rejoice." This, in a nutshell, would be Lincoln's later view, and it was directly related to his effort to seek the truth revealed through the Declaration of Independence and the Constitution. Perhaps the faith of Lincoln, and his nation, were moving on a similar path.

The Impact of Willie's Death on Lincoln's Faith

Lincoln's relationship with members of the nation's faiths likely had some indirect influence on his own faith perspective, but the death of the Lincolns' eleven-year-old son, Willie, struck the president at a far deeper level.

Willie became ill in early February 1862, and his fever, which could have been caused by typhoid, smallpox, or tuberculosis, was so severe it made him delirious. When Tad, the youngest son, also fell ill, the president tended both boys, sitting by their beds night after night. On February 20, Willie died.

Dr. Phineas D. Gurley, the Lincoln family's Presbyterian minister in Washington, was at his bedside at the end. He had been called by Edwin Stanton, when it was clear Willie was close to death, and Mary Lincoln asked Dr. Gurley to perform funeral services at the

White House. Compounding the unbearable horrors of the war, Lincoln and his family had to live through the worst nightmare that parents could imagine.

A remarkable child, whom the president once described fondly as "a very gentle and amiable boy," Willie was a favorite with those who knew him, and his parents felt their son's loss acutely. It came as a visceral blow. At the lengthy funeral and afterward, Lincoln confessed, "This is the hardest trial of my life. Why is it? Oh, why is it?" Mary, confined to her bed, did not attend the funeral, while Lincoln was inconsolable. Frequently, he became so convulsed with grief he hid his face in his hands and sobbed uncontrollably. On several occasions, he asked, "Will I see my boy soon?"

A number of authors have argued that Willie's death had a profound influence on Lincoln's faith. Mary Lincoln noted that afterward, Lincoln "reflected more intently on the ways of God." By 1864, Lincoln had turned to reading scripture intensively. In this return to an interest that hearkened back to his youth, it is likely that Lincoln read the Bible through a slightly different lens, reflecting the influence of Presbyterian pastor James A. Smith and perhaps the modified Calvinism that Smith and Lincoln had discussed during Lincoln's later years in Springfield. His spiritual path in the aftermath of Willie's death was seemingly shifting as he grappled with the great issues of his presidency.

Mary's response moved in a different direction. After Willie's passing, Mary called on the medium Nettie Coburn Maynard to hold séances in the White House. Whether Lincoln attended is uncertain. In *Was Abraham Lincoln a Spiritualist? or, Curious Revelations from the Life of a Trance Medium*, Maynard describes numerous meetings with Lincoln—during which he praised her as having a "very singular gift "—but she admitted that Mrs. Lincoln was more responsive to her approach than was the president.

Covenant Theory

"All the world's a stage," wrote Shakespeare, "and all the men and women merely players." In a strange sense, most people in the seventeenth-century Elizabethan and Stuart world behaved as if they were "on stage." They dressed according to social rank, and every special occasion they attended demanded an elaborate show of formal ceremony. The Catholic church and the Church of England harbored the most elaborate rituals, with ceremonies that marked all the milestones of life: baptism, confirmation, communion, entering Holy Orders, confession, marriage, and, ultimately, death. Similar ceremonies marked the shifts of seasons and major national holidays. But that would soon change in the societies formed by immigrants such as Lincoln's ancestor Samuel Lincoln, a weaver's apprentice from Norfolk Country, East Anglia, who sailed across the Atlantic and settled in Higham, Massachusetts, during the Puritan "Great Migration" of 1630–42.

Samuel Lincoln and other Puritans who moved to New England, like the Scots and English who immigrated to northern Ireland (the Scots-Irish), rejected these overt ceremonies, arguing that they blocked the path to the religious truth. In their certainty, they replaced these earlier models with what historians call "covenant theory." According to the covenant theory of these Puritans, God had made a divine promise to his people (often referencing those who had moved to New England) that he would use this special relationship with their community to bring about his will with time. The covenant bound the people to this special relationship with God. While the promise of divine favor or grace was everlasting, if the community ever became unfaithful or disobedient, it would suffer punishment.

In accepting covenant theory, seventeenth-century New Englanders thereby discarded virtually all the ceremonial rituals of their ancestors. The Puritans saw themselves as unique. They reduced the seven sacraments of the Catholic church and the Church of England to two—baptism and the Lord's Supper—and they also dismissed their ancestors' ceremonies of Christmas and Easter. In essence, they were trying to live their lives, both morally and socially, without ritual.

But no society can survive without ritual. Over the years, colonial New Englanders, such as the Lincolns, created a special set of ceremonies to replace those of the Church of England, which they had dismissed; all of the new rituals were grounded in covenant theory. The first of these emerged as the ceremony of thanksgiving, which gave the people an opportunity to thank God for his blessing of abundance. Equally important was the emergence of a ceremony that acknowledged the moment when man went awry: a ritual of fasting and humiliation. Forming two sides of the same coin fashioned by early seventeenth-century colonials and continued by later generations during the era of the American Revolution, these rituals became known as the New England ceremonies of thanksgiving and fasting and humiliation. Further, they emerged as *the* community symbols of the region. After the Revolution, the legacy of Puritan ceremonies expressing the people's covenant with God soon spread across the North and the South to become the symbols of the new Republic. And in time, these ceremonies also shaped the emerging religious world of the descendant of the weaver's apprentice from Norfolk County, Abraham Lincoln.

Days of Fasting and of Thanksgiving during the Civil War

During the Civil War, both North and South held almost the same number of official days of thanksgiving (after victories) and fasting and humiliation (usually after defeats). Yet today this form of public ceremony, with its deep roots in the nation's colonial past, has disappeared from American life. In August 1945, at the end of World War II, President Truman called for an official day of thanksgiving and remembrance. That momentous occasion marked the last official day acknowledging a recognized, Puritan-based public ceremony introduced during the Civil War and shared by the people, those whose lives have formed the bedrock of American history.

That the Confederacy and the Union would virtually match such commemorations showed the prominence of covenant theory, for both sides subscribed to variant versions of these ceremonial rituals of thanksgiving and fasting, reflecting a theological position that was not as much physical as verbal. Reinforcing a cultural shift that wove its way into their societies, colonial Americans, such as Lincoln's ancestors, had generally decided against borrowing many of the ceremonies linked with Britain, Ireland, and the European continent. The colonials had failed to reenact religious processions, fiestas, maypoles, St. Valentine's Day ceremonies, and Mardi Gras or other wild carnivals that celebrated the overturning of class society. Instead, the colonials had chosen ceremonies centered on verbal expression—days of feasting and days of fasting and humiliation. This collective acknowledgment of a nation in special relationship with God, one that had been carried over from Samuel Lincoln's era, proved much a part of Abraham Lincoln's nineteenth-century world.

During the course of the war, the Confederacy held eight days of thanksgiving or humiliation, and the Union recognized even more. In addition, various southern states stressed their own special days. As these were widely broadcast, both North and South would have been well aware of the situation on the other side of the battle lines. In a deeper sense, the days of thanksgiving and of humiliation represented a collective response to the idea that a sacred cosmos somehow oversaw the destinies of the respective sides. In fact, the first such day of "fasting and prayer" was called by Jefferson Davis on June 14, 1861. On August 12 of that year, when Lincoln issued his first call for public humiliation, fasting, and prayer, he selected the last Thursday in September. He chose Thursday for pragmatic reasons: he hoped to include everyone, and Thursday did not conflict with the day of worship of any group.

The year 1863 saw two more calls by Lincoln for fasting, along with a special day of prayer (April 30) during which the people asked for "the pardon of our natural sins." During that summer of massive carnage on the battlefield, Lincoln also selected the date of August 6 as a day of thanks for the victory at Gettysburg and as a time for Americans to call upon God "to subdue the anger which has produced and so long sustained a needless and cruel rebellion." Amid an atmosphere charged with emotion, Sarah Josepha Hale convinced Lincoln to proclaim the last Thursday in November 1863 as the first annual national Thanksgiving. A special hymn, "Give Thanks, All Ye People," was penned for the occasion, although it soon dropped into obscurity.

Although Thanksgiving won out, the other former public ceremonial day—of fasting and humiliation—failed to retain the nation's attention. With these ceremonial moments, there also came a sense of uncertainty. Would alerting the people to declarations of public prayer and would the energies widely expressed on those days make any difference in the outcome of the war? Did the Puritans' covenant with God still hold for the nation? Just before the 1864 election, James Scovel told Lincoln that God was on their side. Lincoln's reply was not encouraging: "And are you sure that the Lord is on our side? I sometimes doubt it."

Lincoln had a notorious secular streak, and if he retained a lingering doubt, which perhaps cannot be completely ignored, it might be possible to reduce it to the level of the subconscious. This sense of doubt reflects what Allen C. Guelzo calls the "paradox of Lincoln's fatalism." Lincoln could observe, on the one hand, that "the purposes of the Almighty are perfect and must prevail"; on the other hand, when accumulated disasters led Lincoln to despair, Guelzo notes that "he frequently surrendered to a sense of helplessness in the face of an inscrutable cosmic will."

Wrestling with Prayer

Lincoln's well-honed comment from his New Salem days, that "what is to be [will be] and no cares (prayers) of ours will alter the degree," reflected the "ultra Calvinism" of his youth. By the time President-elect Lincoln boarded the train from Springfield for Washington in 1861, he appeared to have modified this position. His farewell address in Springfield called for his nation's prayers, and abundant evidence indicates that Lincoln prayed often during the war years. John Nicolay noted that Lincoln frequently asked people to pray for him. When informed that he was daily remembered in prayer, "not to be heard of men," he said, "Yes, I like that phrase, not to be heard of men." In a letter to Quaker Eliza Gurney, Lincoln wrote, "I am much indebted to the good Christian people of the country for their constant prayers and consolations; and to no one of them, more than to yourself." On one occasion, Lincoln mentioned that he prayed, often daily. Noah Brooks said, "Sometimes it was only ten words, but those ten words he had."

Lincoln also attended Pastor Phineas Gurley's Wednesday prayer meetings—where he sat inconspicuously out of sight in the pastor's study—so that he could hear others' supplications. Lincoln was raised amid poor but good people, and an essential part of the Ohio Valley frontier life of his youth involved prayer. Perhaps his appreciation could be traced to this inherent, deeply rooted admiration for the poor of the world and their unending struggles, wherein prayer accompanied desperate need.

Lincoln also admonished others for failing in their prayer duties. On one occasion, Dr. Morris J. Raphall, a distinguished New York rabbi, came to Washington to request a promotion for his son to the rank of first lieutenant. Lincoln met them and then said, "As God's minister is it not your first duty to be at home today to pray with your people for the success of our army as is being done in every loyal church throughout the North, East and West?" The rabbi blushed and said his assistant was so doing. That is different, said Lincoln. After promoting the son, Lincoln then said, "Now doctor, you can go home and do your own praying."

After the 1864 election, he confessed to Noah Brooks that the prayers of the people had sustained him greatly. But what did prayer mean in Lincoln's world, and for him specifically? (Remember that prayer after an especially dark night of the soul is the most intimate conversation one can have.)

In chapter 4 of *Abraham Lincoln: Theologian of American Anguish*, Elton Trueblood has given a probing assessment of Lincoln's understanding of the role of prayer. As far as can be known, Lincoln did not blame the South, or the southern clergy, who were praying equally fervently for another outcome. Instead of asking God for victory, Lincoln, Trueblood argues, was engaged in a *conversation* with God.

As noted earlier, Lincoln noticeably increased his reading of scripture during the war years, especially after Willie's death. Probing the role of prayer in people's lives, noted biblical scholar Moshe Greenberg once analyzed every instance of prayer in the Bible. Upon completion of this study, Greenberg concluded that people's praying expressed "a vehicle of, an expression of un-self sufficiency." As Lincoln himself phrased it, "I have been driven many times upon my knees by the overwhelming conviction that I had nowhere else to go. My own wisdom and that of all about me seemed insufficient for that day."

Greenberg also noted that it was not just Hebrew priests or leaders who called on God in prayer. In the Bible, a great many of those who prayed were simply common people. In a sense, Lincoln filled both roles. During the years 1861–65, Lincoln was simultaneously the supreme leader of the nation as well as the supreme common person from Illinois, and he had been elevated to the office of the president by the will of the people.

From Lincoln's perspective, the war did not "just happen." Rather, it was a "terrible visitation" from Providence for purposes yet unknown. Lincoln believed he must try to reconcile the two. Thus, when Lincoln prayed, he was searching for a way to merge the persistent Union defeats and setbacks with his own understanding of covenant theory and the words of scripture. His most famous statement along these lines, discovered later by Lincoln biographers Nicolay and Hay, acknowledges that the cosmic will that determines the "contest" between North and South shall "proceed"; cosmic will prevails; and humans will effect God's purpose:

> The will of God prevails. In great contests each party claims to act in accordance with the will of God. Both *may* be and one *must* be wrong. God cannot be *for*, and *against* the same thing at the same time. In the present civil war it is quite possible that God's purpose is something different from the purpose of either party—and yet the human instrumentalities, working just as they do, are of the best adaptation to effect His purpose. I am almost ready to say this is probably true; that God wills this contest, and wills that it shall not end yet. By his mere quiet power on the minds of the now contestants, He could have either *saved* or *destroyed* the Union without a human contest. Yet the contest began. And having begun He could give the final victory to either side any day. Yet the contest proceeds.

Prayer and Emancipation

Lincoln's awareness of the role of prayer and the people's covenant with God, or God's will, had a direct impact on his thoughts on emancipation in early 1863. According to L. E. Christensen, as early as 1861, Lincoln agonized aloud and frequently about the poverty and ruin that the emancipation of the slaves would have on the South. He favored the scheme to pay slave owners through government-financed emancipation so as to lessen the burden on the owners. But in the early months of the war, the position on slavery that he expressed to Congress remained ambiguous because he could not address slavery in the South and slavery in the border states in one voice. Although he worked tirelessly to get the border states—Maryland, Delaware, Kentucky, and Missouri—to free their slaves on their own with federal help, even Delaware, with fewer than two thousand slaves, refused to pass such a law.

Whether God spoke to Lincoln in a "still, small voice" in prayer remains an enigma, but as Trueblood notes, Lincoln well understood that the world often revolves around the friction between complex and flawed systems. In this instance, the choice lay between the destruction of southern society and the emancipation of a downtrodden people. Both covenant theory and the message of scripture seemed to favor the common people. This meant emancipation.

The official wording of the Emancipation Proclamation spoke in terms of "military necessity," although Lincoln also invoked "the considerate judgment of mankind and the gracious favor of Almighty God." It was phrased as a legal document, as, indeed, it was intended to be. But hidden behind the legal and logical argument of military necessity rested Lincoln's cosmic view of the world, and it was his cosmic view that impelled him to this course of action. The introduction of emancipation, according to the diary of Gideon Welles, occurred as follows: On September 22, 1862, Lincoln assembled the cabinet and explained that before the Battle of Antietam he had made a vow, a covenant, that if God gave the Union a victory in the forthcoming battle (Antietam, September 17, 1862), he would consider this victory a manifestation of God's will and move toward emancipation. Although the victory at Antietam was not clear-cut, it had served as an answer to Lincoln's earlier vow. At the cabinet meeting, held several days after the battle, Lincoln noted that it might seem strange that he had submitted the disposal of matters when he was not clearer in his mind about what to do, but he later said, "God had decreed this question in favor of the slaves."

The diary of Salmon P. Chase corroborated this account. According to Chase, Lincoln said—with a slight hesitation in his voice—that he had promised his Maker that if the Union forces were victorious, he would free the slaves.

Then came the preliminary Emancipation Proclamation, followed by the full proclamation issued on January 1, 1863. In Lincoln's view, God, working through history, had taken the position for the furthering of the underclass, a position that one so often finds in scripture.

When the artist Francis B. Carpenter complimented the President on the Emancipation Proclamation as the most sublime moral event in American history, Lincoln said, "Yes . . . as affairs have turned, it is the central act of my administration, and the great event of the nineteenth century." And in terms of military necessity, it was directly related to Lincoln's religious view of the world.

Lincoln's Public Addresses

After the Confederate defeat, General Grant asked, "Mr. President, did you at any time doubt the final success of the cause?" Lincoln replied, "Never for a moment." Generations later, Albert Einstein, in a famous phrase, once said that God does not play dice with the universe.

Lincoln's world was not Einstein's. Even though their lives were divided by only a few decades, the two worlds they inhabited were immeasurably separated. Because the nineteenth-century world was imbued with the concept of national reformation, a truly reformed nation must want that which is just. The moral tone of mid-nineteenth-century America echoes in Lincoln's speeches to the nation and especially in his messages to Congress.

That moral tone appears in the closing statement of the annual message to Congress that the president delivered on December 3, 1861: "The struggle of today is not altogether for today—it is for a vast future also. With a reliance on Providence, let us proceed in the great task which events have devolved upon us." This message anticipates the words Lincoln would deliver a little over three years later in the Second Inaugural Address.

The Second Annual Message to Congress, 1862

In this address, Lincoln urged gradual compensation to pay for emancipation via the Constitution. This method, he assured Congress, would end the war. In his closing, the tone of his speech reached what Michael Burlingame has termed "the soaring rhetoric so conspicuously absent from the legalistic Emancipation Proclamation." Reflecting other aspects of his political position, the message also spoke to the nuanced changes in Lincoln's religion:

> The fiery trial through which we pass, will light us down, in honor or dishonor, to the latest generation. We *say* we are for the Union. The world will not forget that we say this. We know how to save the Union. The world knows we do know how to save it. We—even *we here*—hold the power, and bear the responsibility. In *giving* freedom to the *slave*, we *assure* freedom to the *free*—honorable alike in what we give, and what we preserve. We shall nobly save, or meanly lose, the last best hope of earth.

Here in a nutshell is a restatement of Lincoln's understanding of the goals of the American Revolution, propounded once again in the president's Second Annual Message.

The Gettysburg Address

On Thursday, November 19, 1863, Abraham Lincoln strode across a makeshift wooden platform in Gettysburg, Pennsylvania, to deliver the 272 words that have since become immortal. Countless school children have memorized them, and in *Lincoln at Gettysburg*, Garry Wills argues that with this speech Lincoln essentially reconfigured the ultimate purpose of the ongoing American experiment. The first full-length book on the address appeared in 1930—Bruce Barton's *Lincoln at Gettysburg*—and recently some of the foremost Lincoln scholars of our day have taken up the mantle in their works: see Gabor Boritt's *The Gettysburg Gospel: The Lincoln Speech That Nobody Knows*; Douglas L. Wilson's *Lincoln's Sword: The Presidency and the Power of Words*; and Ronald C. White's *The Eloquent President: A Portrait of Lincoln through His Words*.

To fully comprehend the address, however, one needs to turn to A. E. Elmore, professor of law and English at Athens State University in Alabama. In his book *Lincoln's Gettysburg Address*, Elmore's goal is to present the address as Lincoln intended it to be heard and as his immediate hearers/readers would (probably) have understood it. The current interpretation of the address suggests that Lincoln modeled his speech along classical lines, such as Pericles's famed oath to the dead at Athens. Elmore disagrees. He argues that the president shaped his address by borrowing heavily from two sources that lay much closer to his hearers: the King James Version of scripture and the Protestant Episcopal Church's Book of Common Prayer. Except among the large Roman Catholic minority, the KJV was the most common version of the Bible then in circulation. (Indeed, the Latter-day Saints still consider it the only acceptable translation.) Although less well known, the Episcopal Book of Common Prayer is a 364-page volume that restates many scriptural passages and also contains liturgical readings for such milestones as baptism, marriage, burial, and the dedication of a church. During his youth, Lincoln memorized numerous passages from the KJV, and Elmore believes that he could have also done so from the Book of Common Prayer. When he occasionally attended Episcopal services in Springfield with Mary Todd in the 1840s, copies of the prayer book lay in every pew.

During the Civil War era, politics, religion, and sacred language overlapped on a variety of fronts, as in the days of prayers and fasting called by the governments in both the North and South. Common phrases that had spilled over from an earlier America, such as "the apple of his eye" and "a land flowing with milk and honey," were all biblically based and had retained their popularity. Many people felt as close to the figures in the Old and New Testaments as they did to their distant neighbors. Allusions to the Bible were omnipresent.

In the twenty-first century, many Americans have difficulty comprehending this sensibility. Social critics have noted a rapid rise in "biblical illiteracy" as the terminology of popular culture has largely replaced the role of scripture, once the major source of shared metaphors. Within the halls of colleges and universities, the predominance of deconstructionism (which Elmore terms "worthless flotsam") has contributed to this dilemma, as has the pervasiveness of cinema, video, and the Internet, which have gained renown for their simplistic portrayals of both character and language. As a result, many contemporary Americans find themselves baffled by a speech that reverberates on both political and sacred levels. But, Elmore argues convincingly, by echoing both the KJV and the Book of Common Prayer, this was precisely what Lincoln did with his famed address.

Lincoln's controlling metaphor revolved around the theme of the birth, death, and rebirth of the nation, and this resonated with his audience as a parallel with the birth, death, and rebirth of Jesus. Similarly, Lincoln's reference to "our fathers" recalled not just Washington, Jefferson, and Adams but also Jesus's heavenly and earthly fathers, Jehovah and Joseph. Likewise, the key phrases "brought forth," "conceived," and "dedicated" can be found, in that precise order, in the Book of Common Prayer's litany for the Public Baptism of Infants. As Jesus was conceived, brought forth, and dedicated to serve humankind, so too, Lincoln implied, was the United States conceived, brought forth, and dedicated to the Jeffersonian ideal that "all men are created equal." And, of course, the famous word "fourscore" comes directly from Psalm 90: "The days of our years are threescore years and ten; and if by reason of strength they be fourscore years, yet is their strength labour and sorrow; for it is soon cut off, and we fly away."

The parallels continue. The phrase "we are met" echoes the Book of Common Prayer marriage ceremony phrase "we are gathered"; so too does Lincoln's tendency to couple words—"so conceived and so dedicated," "fitting and proper"—reflect the language of the prayer book. "His echoes of the Prayer Book are every bit as clear and insistent as his echoes of the King James Bible," Elmore notes, "just not quite as frequent." Elmore has also discovered that only 3 of the 272 words—"proposition," "civil," as in "civil war," and "detract"—are *not* present in either the KJV or the Book of Common Prayer. This is an absolutely stunning interpretation.

If Elmore is correct in his interpretation, the Gettysburg Address looms as a central doctrine of Lincoln's religious-political outlook on the world. The covenant between Providence and the American nation, rooted in the colonial experience, remained in place. The goal of the American nation remained to bring it to fulfillment.

Elmore's dual disciplines of law and English are both reflected in his analysis. For example, he devotes entire chapters to semi-legalistic discussions of the phrases "dedicate-consecrate-hallow," "fitting and proper," "dedicated to the proposition," and "under God." He similarly draws on logic and reason as much as on empirical historical evidence to argue that Lincoln's restatement of Jefferson's "all men are created equal" emerged as a deliberate reply to recent southern Presbyterian/northern Episcopal pamphlet restatements of John C. Calhoun's attack on the idea as a glittering generality. Elmore also emphasizes the fact that the phrase "new birth," as in "new birth of freedom," does not appear at all in the KJV but is found twice in the Book of Common Prayer. But to seek out a literary source for every one of Lincoln's sentences is to overlook the considerable presence of oral history in the president's own life. Lincoln's Ohio River Valley world still had one foot in the Anglo-Celtic/American oral culture during the nineteenth century, and surely Lincoln had already heard the phrase "new birth" a number of times before he read it in the Book of Common Prayer, if indeed he ever did.

Elmore also suggests that contemporary Episcopalians would likely have recognized Lincoln's borrowing from the prayer book. (In fact, Elmore himself did so as a young man.) Unlike the Baptists, the Methodists, and the Presbyterians, who split into northern and southern groups before the Civil War, the Episcopal church (about 160,000 members, the sixth largest in the nation) did not officially divide over the issue of slavery. Still, relations between northern and southern Episcopal churches essentially ceased for the duration of the war. Numerous Confederate officers, and several members of Jefferson Davis's cabinet, including Davis himself, were Episcopal church adherents; but so too were William Henry Seward, Salmon P. Chase, and Gideon Welles of Lincoln's cabinet. Ohio Episcopal bishop Charles P. McIlvaine visited England several times, seeking to strengthen the Union cause among Church of England officials. Although these churchmen might well have heard echoes of the prayer book in the Gettysburg Address, it is doubtful that Lincoln's words would have resonated with them on the same level.

Elmore's suggestion that Abraham Lincoln deliberately drew from these two majestic literary sources to reach out to a Catholic-Baptist-Methodist-Episcopal-Presbyterian-Quaker-Jewish audience is both thoughtful and exceptionally well argued. Whether one agrees with his interpretation or not, this is a genuinely provocative thesis. Indeed, after one ponders Elmore's analysis, it becomes impossible to read the Gettysburg Address in the same light again. Elmore's persuasive theory reminds us of the powerful role that "mere words" played in the American Civil War.

The Second Inaugural Address

In the wee hours of the morning of November 9, 1864, Lincoln heard the news of his victory in the presidential election. Shortly thereafter, he spoke informally to a group of supporters, observing: "I give thanks to the Almighty for this evidence of the people's resolution to stand by free government and the rights of humanity." In that brief moment of triumph, the moral tone that highlighted Lincoln's formal state papers appeared again. Even in these spontaneous remarks, that tone was present. It had become part of his persona, and it would reappear in the words of the Second Inaugural Address.

About five weeks before his assassination, Lincoln delivered this speech to Congress. The many observers who have commented on this address have, almost invariably, focused on its final sentences. As Michael Burlingame notes, the concluding words of this speech have become "the most revered and beloved" and have "brought tears to many eyes," resonating with Lincoln's audiences because his crafting of these thoughts seems to have encapsulated the heart of the message that emerged during his presidency. But for those who read them after his assassination, and for the later generations who have viewed them within the mythos of America's past, they have retained a lingering poignancy:

> Fondly do we hope—fervently do we pray—that this mighty scourge of war may speedily pass away. Yet, if God wills that it

continue . . . so still it must be said "the judgments of the Lord are true and righteous altogether." With malice toward none; with charity for all; with firmness in the right, as God gives us to see the right, let us strive on to finish the work we are in; to bind up the nation's wounds; to care for him who shall have borne the battle, and for his widow, and his orphan—to do all which may achieve and cherish a just, and a lasting peace among ourselves, and with all nations.

Contemporaries were astonished with the address. Carl Schurz called the Second Inaugural "a sacred poem." Schurz observed that "no American President had ever spoken words like these to the American people." In a similar vein, Noah Brooks said of the Second Inaugural that it was "as truly a religious document as a state paper." Frederick Douglass, whose arrival at the White House gathering following the inaugural led to a stunningly difficult moment for such an auspicious figure, also reflected on the spiritual tone of the address, characterizing it as a "sacred effort." Burlingame notes that the renowned African American thought it "sounded more like a sermon than like a state paper."

In a recent assessment of the Second Inaugural, Allen Guelzo observes that the full document indicates the paradox in Lincoln's life. For Guelzo, "Lincoln the 'fatalist,' who had no assurance that the will of any person was free, is also the great giver of liberty, the emancipator of millions and the rebuilder of a sundered Republic." Guelzo continues, "There seems no easy way to reconcile the man who believed that all human action was decided by powers beyond human control, and the president who reiterated his faith in the capacity of individuals to improve themselves via a free-labor system which 'gives hope to all, and energy, and progress, and improvement of condition to all.'" Guelzo concludes, "It was precisely Lincoln's embrace of paradox—of both 'necessity' and the 'right to rise'—which granted him both the deterministic stability and the self-willed initiative to save the Republic from the greatest challenge it would face." By embracing the Second Inaugural in its entirety, Guelzo reminds us of why Lincoln—a man of spiritual complexity and frontier tenacity—has endured as the subject of such extended commentary.

In a further commentary on Lincoln's faith, it remains an interesting coincidence that one of the last acts of Congress that President Lincoln signed in the late winter of 1864–65 expanded the use of the motto "In God we trust," an inscription initially designated for the one-cent and two-cent coins. With Lincoln's signature, this motto would soon appear on all national coins.

These last months of Lincoln's life that coincided with the final months of the war raise once again the question of Lincoln's religious faith. Noah Brooks related a story that may offer some insight into the matter. In an article in *Harper's Magazine*, Brooks told this story about Lincoln and one of his meetings with persistent members of the public who sought his assistance:

> On Thursday of a certain week, two ladies, from Tennessee, came before the President, asking the release of their husbands, held as prisoners of war at Johnson's Island. They were put off until Friday, when they came again, and were again put off until Saturday. At each of the interviews one of the ladies urged that her husband was a religious man. On Saturday, when the President ordered the release of the prisoner, he said to this lady, "You say your husband is a religious man; tell him, when you meet him that I say I am not much of a judge of religion, but that in my opinion the religion which sets men to rebel and fight against their Government, because, as they think, that Government does not sufficiently help *some* men to eat their bread in the sweat of *other* men's faces, is not the sort of religion upon which people can get to heaven."

Summary

This chapter has traced Lincoln's religious perspective from the convoluted journey to Washington in February 1861 through the Second Inaugural in March 1865, an address in which his words succeeded in merging any clear distinction between a formal state paper and a commentary on religion. The Second Inaugural proved the capstone of Lincoln's search for the elusive meaning of the nation's never-ending war and also marked a culminating moment of the emerging religious world that he came to understand during his presidency.

The initial shaping of Lincoln's religious understanding may have been rooted within the Ohio River Valley of Kentucky, Indiana, and Illinois, but his years in the White House led him to reconsider that formative perspective, and the views he carried from the Ohio Valley to the nation's capital did not hold up under the barrage of blows that struck him between 1861 and 1865.

Lincoln's relationship with the various faiths of America reinforced his ecumenism and his genuine fairness in acknowledging religious equality and humanistic concerns, whether among Quakers who lived out their pacifist beliefs during the war or among Native Americans whose faith evoked so little sympathy from other Americans. But it was the loss of Willie that compounded the brutality of war at a very personal level. With Willie's death, it seemed the battlefield had come into the Lincolns' home, bringing with it the unanswered questions "Why is it? Oh, why is it?"

The adaptation of covenant theory into the milieu of the Civil War moved the president another step toward the religious world that he was beginning to comprehend. The days of thanksgiving and humiliation and fasting reinforced Lincoln's growing perception that the American Republic was a nation in a special relationship with God. In this charged atmosphere, his own praying intensified, and he observed that he had "been driven many times by the overwhelming conviction that I had nowhere else to go. My own wisdom and that of all about me seemed insufficient for that day."

As Lincoln's religious perceptions shifted, the "conversation" that he engaged in with God alerted the president to the potential for messages from the Almighty. In September 1862, when Lincoln accepted the Union victory at the Battle of Antietam as a sign from God for the issuing of the preliminary Emancipation Proclamation, he told members of the cabinet about the vow or covenant he had made with God. Later he observed that "God had decreed this question in favor of the slaves." The decision for emancipation came directly from Lincoln's emerging views on religion and his increasing "reliance on Providence."

The president's state papers and addresses that followed the free-ing of the slaves—especially the Gettysburg Address and the Second Inaugural—drove home the concepts of freedom and equality that propelled this magisterial gesture; further, they intensified the moral tone of a nation reborn through reform and civil war. As Lincoln ob-served in his Second Annual Message to Congress in 1862, delivered just a few months after the preliminary Emancipation Proclamation, "We shall nobly save, or meanly lose, the last best hope of earth." But for Lincoln, the resolution of America's destiny—whether it be saved or lost—rested in "the judgments of the Lord." The president-elect who had stepped onto the train in Springfield in early 1861 had finally come to terms with the Almighty, a "God working through history."

First Presbyterian Church, Springfield, Illinois. The Lincolns attended this church before they moved to Washington, D.C. Courtesy of the archives of the First Presbyterian Church of Springfield, Illinois.

Reverend Dr. James A. Smith, pastor of First Presbyterian Church, Springfield, Illinois. Lincoln and Smith developed a close friendship. Courtesy of the archives of the First Presbyterian Church of Springfield, Illinois.

Second Presbyterian Church, Washington, D.C. (also known as New York Avenue Presbyterian Church). The Lincolns attended this church during their years in the capital. Photographer, Margaret Connell Szasz.

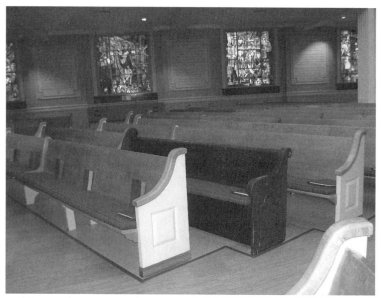

The Lincoln pew, Second Presbyterian Church, Washington, D.C. This is the only pew in the church that has not been altered since Lincoln's presidency. Photographer, Margaret Connell Szasz.

Lincoln's Address at the Dedication of the Gettysburg National Cemetery, November 19, 1863.

Lithograph of Lincoln addressing the crowd at the dedication of the Gettysburg National Cemetery, November 19, 1863. Courtesy of the Library of Congress.

Painting of Lincoln showing Sojourner Truth the Bible presented to him by African Americans of Baltimore, October 29, 1864. Courtesy of the Library of Congress.

Crowd at Lincoln's second inauguration, during which he delivered one of his most enduring addresses, March 4, 1865. Courtesy of the Library of Congress.

Arch at Twelfth Street in Chicago, erected during the long train journey carrying the body of the slain president from the capital to Springfield. The train made many stops, including this one in Chicago, April 1865. Courtesy of the Library of Congress.

Abraham Lincoln, the Martyr, Victorious (ca. 1866, John Sartain, engraver, Philadelphia, 1808–97). Courtesy of the Library of Congress.

Lincoln Memorial, carved by Daniel Chester French and dedicated in 1922. Photographer, Margaret Connell Szasz.

LINCOLN AS THE CENTER OF
AMERICA'S CIVIL RELIGION

Shortly after the assassination of the president, Ralph Waldo Emerson described Lincoln as "the true historian of the American people in his time." And throughout the saga of the Civil War, some people pondered whether he would serve his country even more by his death than with his life. That, of course, is exactly what occurred, as Abraham Lincoln evolved into a new role, becoming the nation's civic father.

When countries around the world heard the news of Lincoln's assassination, their people were shocked. Letters of condolences poured in to the nation's capital. In March 1867, the U.S. Congress passed a resolution to publicly publish this correspondence in a large, seven-hundred-page volume that was then sent to each of the states. The majority of the condolences represent Victorian formality, but they are also very revealing regarding the sentiment of the world in the spring of 1865. Lincoln's observation that the United States represented "the last best hope of earth" found an echo in the resolutions of the working classes of the United Kingdom that rejoiced at "the complete falsification of the statements that American institutions were a failure." The *Dublin Daily Express* said that all Irishmen, regardless of their politics, would regard the assassination as the most horrible catastrophe in history. The consul general at Florence wrote that Lincoln was not just an American, "he was also ours." The Mexican government ordered all civil employees to wear mourning for nine days. Still, nothing in the formal condolences matched the Manchester schoolboys' cheer in the late 1860s. When asked who was the greatest man outside the United Kingdom, the schoolboys shouted loudly, "Abraham Lincoln!" as if he were still alive.

The mythological dimension of Lincoln's life took hold immediately, and, characteristically, the myth has retained its strength through the many generations that have followed. As theologian Reinhold Niebuhr has noted, myth carries far more power than mere facts, for myth touches the transcendent in a way that mere facts cannot reach. According to Lloyd Lewis's *Myths after Lincoln*, the farmers in Illinois swore that the brown thrush did not sing for a full year after Lincoln's assassination. Further, in the 1890s, when Lincoln's log cabin began to attract interest, drawing on the power of his humble roots, the logs that supposedly composed his family's Kentucky home went on a popular nationwide tour. On July 21, 1887, Robert T. Lincoln deeded the family house to the state of Illinois.

Strangely enough, official celebration of Lincoln's February 12 birthday proved irregular. Months after his death, Congress passed a joint resolution calling for a speech marking Lincoln's fifty-seventh birthday on February 12, 1866, but it was not until 1891 that Hannibal Hamlin of Maine (Lincoln's first vice president) began a campaign to turn February 12 into a national holiday. The movement grew slowly, but by the time of Lincoln's centenary, many southern states seemed more than ready to join in.

In 1909, President Theodore Roosevelt, who as a boy had watched Lincoln's cortege move through New York City, declared February 12 a legal holiday in the District of Columbia and U.S. territories. By 1938, at least twenty-seven states also officially celebrated the holiday. In 1971, Congress decided to combine Lincoln's and Washington's birthdays into one holiday, making the third Monday of February Presidents' Day.

Equally important, and supported by the Lincoln Life Insurance Company of Fort Wayne, Indiana, which guided the restoration of Indiana's role in shaping Lincoln's youth, the Boy Scouts began a campaign to march every February 12 to the *Abraham Lincoln: The Hoosier Youth* statue at Fort Wayne's Lincoln Museum for an appropriate ceremony. In 1909, the Lincoln family's log cabin in Kentucky was enshrined in a Grecian-style temple near Hodgenville. The Civilian Conservation Corps' superb restoration of the village of New Salem, Illinois, during the 1930s offered yet another shrine for Lincoln, followed by the 1963 consecration of Lincoln's homestead as Indiana's first national park and the opening of the Abraham Lincoln Presidential Library and Museum in Springfield, Illinois, in 2004 and 2005. Today, one can explore absolutely every step of Lincoln's life from his birthplace to Springfield to Ford's Theatre. This form of reminiscence is not available for any other president, nor is it likely to occur again. Paradoxically, the myth surrounding Lincoln may have made it more difficult to understand the nature of his faith perspective.

Lincoln and America's Civil Religion

In the turbulent 1960s, sociologist Robert Bellah and historian Sydney E. Mead originated the idea—borrowing from Rousseau—that America had a "civil religion." In their essays and speeches, Bellah and Mead argued that the nation had created an authentic faith perspective that runs parallel but not in opposition to the great historic religious faiths of America: Protestantism, Roman Catholicism, and Judaism. This newly crafted civil faith, however, reflects enough "unitarian" emphasis so that it does not offend nonbelievers; further, it is not specific enough to offend the various Christian denominations.

Drawing from Rousseau's social contract regarding the duty of each citizen, this civil religion has its own holy places—the Washington Monument, the Supreme Court Building, the Jefferson Memorial, the White House, and, preeminently, the Lincoln Memorial. It possesses its own collection of secular saints—James Madison, Alexander Hamilton, Thomas Jefferson, Abraham Lincoln, Martin Luther King Jr., and John F. Kennedy. Taught in both parochial and public schools, often by foreign-born instructors, this "faith" has served as the glue that helps the United States, one of the few authentically multi-ethnic nations, to retain its sense of self. Although somewhat reduced now, the concept of America's civil religion will never completely die down.

And at the center of this national civil faith, even in the twenty-first century, strides the figure of Abraham Lincoln. Lincoln has emerged as the transcendental man. Lincoln can show modern minds how to respond in moments of crisis; he is one measure of how Americans should react in times of trouble.

Americans have called on his immense sense of compassion in moments of need, spurred on by Vachel Lindsay's poem "Abraham Lincoln Walks at Midnight." The radical "Lincoln Brigade" fought with the Spanish commandos during the Spanish Civil War of the 1930s. During the 1940s, Robert Sherwood's *Abraham Lincoln in Illinois* remained the classic anti-fascist play of the era. In 2009, the two-hundredth anniversary of Lincoln's birth, despite the economic recession, Lincoln and Lincoln-Darwin conferences were plentiful, for these two renowned men were born on the same day.

No matter how one assesses his life, Abraham Lincoln stands at the very center of the American experience. The growing popularity of comic books in the twentieth century gave the American public yet another medium in which to learn about the sixteenth president, as comic book artists elevated Lincoln as one of their heroes. An untold number of comic books focusing on Lincoln, such as Dell Comics' "Abraham Lincoln Life Story" (1958), taught what it meant to be American, perhaps suggesting that if one knows Abraham Lincoln, one knows America.

And Lincoln as exemplar holds well into the twenty-first century. As then Illinois senator Barack Obama once noted of Lincoln, "In his self-study and ultimate mastery of the language and the law, in his capacity to overcome personal loss and his increased determination in the face of responsibilities—in all of this we see a truncated element of the American character, a belief that we can constantly remake ourselves to fit our larger dreams."

America's civil religion has also boasted its own set of "sacred scriptures," with Lincoln well represented. The Constitution, the Declaration of Independence, the Bill of Rights, the Emancipation Proclamation, and other treasured documents are housed in the National Archives in an atmosphere that Jeffrey F. Meyer likens to the placement of the Torah in the ark of the covenant. In 1947, at the opening of the

Cold War, the American "Freedom Train" carried copies of these "sacred scriptures" on a grand tour around the nation. This enabled Americans living in the far stretches of the continent to see copies of over 175 documents, including Jefferson's copy of the Declaration, the Bill of Rights, and a copy of the Constitution annotated by Washington.

Lincoln's Emancipation Proclamation was included among the documents, and before the Freedom Train began its tour, federal officials insisted that southern cities rescind all segregation laws for visitors to the train. When Birmingham and Memphis refused to do so, the train simply bypassed them.

Even more than the Emancipation Proclamation itself, however, the symbol of America's civil religion emerged in the creation of the Lincoln Memorial.

The Lincoln Memorial

The Lincoln Memorial stands out among all the iconic buildings of Washington, D.C. Indeed, it holds a worldwide recognition comparable to the Capitol Building itself. Far more than the Washington Monument, the Capitol dome, or the Jefferson Memorial, the massive sculpture created by famed artist Daniel Chester French remains an international attraction. Over fifty years in the planning, Congress finally appointed a special Lincoln Memorial Commission to erect a suitable monument in 1911. There were endless discussions on the proper way to memorialize the nation's sixteenth president. The chief resistance to the erection of a giant statue lay in Minnesota representative J. T. McCleary's idea of an Abraham Lincoln memorial highway or "Lincoln Way"—similar to the Appian Way, the ancient Roman highway—stretching from the capital to Gettysburg, Pennsylvania. But that proposal proved too expensive. Finally, over the objection of Speaker of the House Joseph Cannon from Illinois, Congress decided on a gigantic statue that would eventually be carved by sculptor French, whose striking "standing Lincoln" statue (dedicated in 1912), situated on the west side of the capitol at Lincoln, Nebraska, had already gained attention as a tourist attraction. Over the next several years, French and his team erected a massive seated Lincoln within a modified Grecian temple.

In 1922, chief justice of the U.S. Supreme Court (and former president) William Howard Taft presided over the dedication of the memorial, alongside a number of African American dignitaries, who, ironically, were relegated to a separate, segregated section. As Dr. Robert R. Moton, president of Tuskegee Institute (and the successor of Booker T. Washington), noted in his speech, the memorial linked the arrival of two ships that founded the United States—the *Mayflower* in Massachusetts in 1620 and the first slave ship in Jamestown the year before, which brought the institution of slavery to America. Taft noted that the memorial represented a shrine "at which all can worship." As historian Christopher A. Thomas has observed, for most foreign visitors, the Lincoln Memorial has become a metaphor for the entire nation.

This symbolic identification holds true for many citizens as well. After half a century, the most memorable political cartoon commemorating the assassination of John F. Kennedy in 1963 remains Bill Mauldin's depiction of a grieving Lincoln Memorial, portraying Lincoln holding his head in his hands.

But the image of the memorial can be used to celebrate as well. Denied access to the Daughters of the American Revolution facilities, famed African American contralto Marian Anderson held her Easter Sunday open-air concert in front of the memorial in 1939. Twenty-four years later, Martin Luther King delivered his famed "I Have a Dream" speech under its shadow, an event commemorated on its fiftieth anniversary in August 2013. Each of these figures performed before gargantuan crowds. As Jeffrey F. Meyer has observed, the similarity between the son of a carpenter (Jesus) and a rail-splitter (Lincoln) is obvious; perhaps this accounts for the fact that during the Cold War, Dwight Eisenhower was observed praying there.

A recent symbolic use of the memorial occurred when Democratic candidate Barack Obama won the presidential race in November 2008. Once again, political cartoonists had a heyday. Dana Summers of the *Orlando Sentinel* depicted an empty chair with the dialogue, "Where's Lincoln? Not back from Chicago yet." Adam Zyglis of the *Buffalo News* depicted the statue crying from joy; Steve Breen of the *San Diego Union-Tribune* had him beaming; while Mike Keefe of the *Denver Post* and David Fitzsimons of the Arizona *Daily Star* portrayed the statue waving its arms in delight. The story also held a magnetic appeal for foreign cartoonists. Vince O'Farrell of the *Illawarra Mercury* in Australia showed Obama standing on the arm of the statue with the caption "Ready, Willing and Abe."

Lincoln and Coins

During Abraham Lincoln's ascendency in the 1850s, when the nation was redefining itself, the concept of civil religion, later articulated by Bellah and Mead, was being shaped. Lincoln was among those influential figures for whom nationalism had achieved a level of meaning almost equivalent to a religious faith. Lincoln revered the union with a sense of awe approaching religious mysticism, which led to the rise of nationalism as a civil religion. In time, Lincoln himself became a focal point of civil religion, and this was clearly evidenced in his appearance on national coins.

Ever since the founding of the nation, the American Republic had scrupulously avoided placing the image of any president on its coins. Instead, various representatives of liberty or Great Plains Indians (from 1864) had graced the face of U.S. coinage. Traditionally, this representation did not apply to commemorative medals, which often bore presidential images; at least fifty versions of mourning medals were produced in the weeks after Lincoln's death. At the centennial of the nation in 1876, the U.S. Mint issued its own medal, which remained so popular that the mint still sells copies yet today. While the medal does not feature Lincoln, it depicts a stirring image of independence: a female rising from a recumbent position, holding a sword in her right hand, while she raises her left hand to the thirteen stars above her; around the medal are the words "These United Colonies are, and of right ought to be, Free and Independent States."

The first U.S. currency to feature Lincoln was issued as an emergency measure in August 1861. His image also appeared on the admission ticket to the World's Fair held in Chicago in 1893.

By the 1920s, the Lincoln portrait had become a fixture on the five dollar bill, over time shifting through a series of progressive innovations. Five dollars represented a considerable sum of money during the early twentieth century, so not every citizen became overly familiar with it. But that changed in 1909. In that year, Theodore Roosevelt commissioned a Lithuanian immigrant, Victor D. Brenner, to design a special coin for the centennial of Lincoln's birth.

In circulation for over a century, the Lincoln penny, which has crossed the 500 billion mark, ranks as the most popular coin. It is the most reproduced artistic image of any person in all of history. Brenner's artistic rendering of the president—a slightly sad countenance but with the hint of a smile—has become the most common image of Abraham Lincoln.

The Lincoln penny was officially released to the public on August 2, 1909. The Philadelphia mint had stockpiled about 25 million coins for the occasion, but its miscalculation soon became apparent. Within a short time, handmade "No more Lincoln pennies" signs appeared in front of various subtreasury locations. "The common, lonely face of Honest Abe Lincoln looks good on the penny," said writer Carl Sandburg, "the coin of the common folk from whom he came and to whom he belongs."

In the early twentieth century, most children who chose coin collecting as a hobby began in earnest with the appearance of the Lincoln penny. Decades later, in 1959, the sesquicentennial of Lincoln's birth, the reverse side of the penny was reconfigured, and the Lincoln Memorial replaced the Illinois wheat shafts on the original Lincoln penny designed by Frank Gasparro.

At the bicentennial of Lincoln's birth in 2009, the U.S. Mint issued a one-cent coin as part of the formal celebrations. Since pennies cost about three cents each to coin, the mint lost millions on reproducing four new versions: Lincoln's log cabin; Lincoln as rail-splitter; Lincoln in his professional life as a lawyer; and Lincoln in his presidency. On his 201st birthday, the mint issued yet another release, the Union Shield that dated from Civil War times, and this design—the ultimate symbol of Lincoln's preservation of the Union—will replace the far better known memorial for the indefinite future.

Each bicentennial design received a formal launch in various appropriate locations, and the mint hoped that the new reverses would duplicate the popularity of the state quarter series. More than ten thousand rolls of the Lincoln log cabin pennies were sold to collectors on the first day. Professional numismatic companies did a land-office business when they began to sell the various configurations of the coins. One could purchase a roll of fifty Lincoln coins for about $1,000; a special "first day of issue" registry set of four pennies for about $1,600; or a highly regarded log cabin first day of issue for over $3,000.

It would not be too much to say that the humble image of Lincoln who first appeared on a 1909 coin (cost of a roll: fifty cents) has turned into a twenty-first-century symbol of greed for many collectors. The image of Lincoln not only resides at the core of American civil religion but rests at the base of American capitalism as well.

CONCLUSION: THE ENIGMA—
WAS LINCOLN A CHRISTIAN?

At Oak Ridge Cemetery in Springfield, Illinois, on May 4, 1865, Methodist bishop Matthew Simpson delivered a noted eulogy. Admitting that he could not speak "definitely" about Lincoln's faith, he nonetheless observed that Lincoln had "believed in Christ." Lincoln's brother-in-law Ninian Edwards later agreed, and in 1873 James A. Smith, minister of Springfield's First Presbyterian Church, concurred.

Newcomers to the world of Lincoln studies are often surprised at the extraordinary degree of attention devoted to his religious position. Indeed, aside from his views on race and slavery, there is no other field of study that has generated as much attention as Lincoln's religion. Virtually every organized religious group and anti-religious group has claimed Lincoln as "one of them." The Baptists have so done because Lincoln's parents belonged to the church, and during this time Lincoln helped with church activities in the Little Pigeon Creek Baptist Church in Indiana when he was a teenager. The Episcopalian claim on Lincoln is based on the facts that he surely attended Rev. Charles Dresser's services in Springfield when he was courting Mary Todd and during their early life together and that the two were married in an Episcopal ceremony. The Presbyterians note that the Lincolns purchased a pew in James A. Smith's Presbyterian church in Springfield, and they continued to hold that pew until their departure in 1861. After Lincoln and Mary had moved to Washington, they attended Second Presbyterian Church. This church has long maintained a plaque on the pew where Lincoln sat during the services, and it remains the only pew that has not been replaced since 1865.

In a less demonstrative statement, the Quakers have pointed out that Lincoln's ancestors in Pennsylvania were most probably Quaker. After the president's assassination, Rabbi Isaac Mayer Wise declared that Lincoln had told him he believed he was Jewish. The Society for Freethinkers also claimed him for that denomination. Even a Pietist church group stated that Lincoln was intending to join after the war was over, reporting that he was secretly baptized in their faith.

The conflicting claims on Lincoln's loyalty lead back to the central questions: what faith did Lincoln hold, and was he a Christian? Understanding Lincoln's position on this core issue of his life remains one of the many imponderables of the sixteenth president. Hence, any answer to the question retains a baffling complexity.

Although Lincoln never joined any church, he attended services in Baptist, Episcopal, and Presbyterian churches, and these experiences contributed to his cumulative position on the Christian faith. But he was not a bona fide member of any of these denominations. Still, even though he did not join a church, Lincoln absorbed the ethical dimension of Christianity. Ethical teachings, of course, can never be limited to the world of religion. One does not have to search far to find examples of Christians violating their ethical code. And, at the same time, many nonbelievers can behave ethically. Although the dispute about what Lincoln actually believed shows no sign of resolution, there is virtually no disagreement that he lived his life through a structure rooted in a Christian ethical framework.

After Lincoln's assassination, his early biographers claimed he was a Christian, but the indefatigable and mercurial William Herndon spent a great deal of time and effort trying to prove that Lincoln thought exactly like he did, as a nonconventional religious thinker, perhaps an atheist or at least an agnostic, or (at best) a vague sort of mixture of Unitarian/Universalist (as Herndon himself later became). Herndon's invaluable collection of statements from people who had known Lincoln from his New Salem days supplied plenty of ammunition to support the idea that Lincoln was a religious skeptic.

One New Salem acquaintance said Lincoln was an atheist, while another repeated numerous times that Lincoln was a "Southern Baptist," citing Lincoln's parents' affiliation with the Baptist church. James H. Mahoney, the New Salem freethinker, claimed that two of Robert Burns's poems—"Address to the Unco Guid, or Rigidly Righteous" and "Holy Willie's Prayer"—that offered a satirical comment on the Presbyterian Church of Scotland expressed Lincoln's views on religion during the time Mahoney had known him in New Salem. Yet those who knew Lincoln during his years in Washington discerned the views of a leader who was coming to terms with the Almighty.

When Herndon interviewed Mary Todd Lincoln, she admitted that "technically" Lincoln was not a Christian. By "technically" she meant that Lincoln had never undergone a conversion experience or officially joined a nonevangelical church, such as the Episcopal church.

Is it possible to determine if Lincoln was a Christian? The comments of his contemporaries seem to indicate a huge discrepancy of opinion. Perhaps the amorphous quality of Protestantism accounts for these discrepancies. Given Protestantism's dispersed nature, it cannot support a centralized body that can determine precisely whether a person is or is not a "Christian." Although Lincoln often spoke as if in prayer, still one might ask: were the words he uttered the prayer of a Christian? The question persists. One can say that a person is or is not a Roman Catholic; is or is not a Methodist; is or is not a Latter-day Saint; but there is no polity, no structure, no single institution that assumes this decision-making authority for Protestants in general, nor for the entirety of "Christians."

And surely Lincoln behaved in a manner that led his contemporaries to agree that his actions befitted those of a Christian. He fought a war without maligning the South. He was responsible for the freeing of the slaves. And, when peace arrived, all he asked of the South was repentance and a willingness to return to the Union.

As president of the United States, Lincoln pardoned hundreds of soldiers for various offenses during the war; indeed, he pardoned so many that several officers feared the weakening of army discipline. In the same frame of mind, Lincoln hoped that Jefferson Davis would escape so as to avoid a long trial. And he was a steady pursuer of social justice against the most prominent evil of the day. It was clear to Lincoln: "If slavery is not wrong, then nothing is wrong." And he concluded that God had decided on a mission to end slavery.

During the war itself, the president gave some indication of the position toward the South that he would adopt when the war had ended. In December 1863, Lincoln issued an amnesty proclamation offering pardons, granted on condition of taking an oath to support the Constitution and to obey the laws of the United States and the presidential proclamation with regard to slavery and freedom. The Amnesty Proclamation was severely critiqued for its stance on the nature of the pardon that it offered. This proclamation argued that "when a man is sincerely *penitent* for his misdeeds and gives satisfactory evidence of the same, he can surely be pardoned, and there is no exception to the rule."

Francis B. Carpenter, who lived in the White House for several months, said of Lincoln that he believed no man had a more abiding sense of his dependence on God and a belief in the ultimate triumph of truth and right in the world. As the Great Emancipator, Lincoln's most enduring legacy brought these qualities to his decision to free the slaves. During the 1858 debates with Stephen Douglas, Lincoln had made quite clear his position on slavery and moral neutrality. Because Americans now acknowledge the inherent evil of slavery, especially since the civil rights movement, the Emancipation Proclamation has lost some of its luster in the great panoply of America's sacred documents. Perhaps it should be restored to its rightful place. When Lincoln wrote the proclamation, he phrased it in legal, war-related terms—rather than moral ones—so that, if needed, it could be challenged in the court system. Lincoln knew well that purposeful, pious statements have no legal bearing in the law. He also knew that this was undeniably a moral issue. That he let Providence decide on the issuing of the Emancipation Proclamation indicated the precise moment when he showed his faith in the inherent moral righteousness of a covenanted universe. That this was not the Deistic world of his youth is thus clearly evident. The Lincoln who was at home in the antebellum world of the Ohio Valley was not the Lincoln of 1861–65.

As Henry Horner has shrewdly observed, Lincoln "matured slowly." Once the nation had plunged into war and Lincoln had assumed the leadership of that nation, he was no longer able to reach independent decisions. He saw God as holding the deciding hand, and he himself could not know how that would play out. Further, the overwhelming burden of the war, mixed with Lincoln and Mary's personal losses and his continued faith quest, changed the rules of the game. During his presidency, Lincoln had moved into a world beholden to Providence.

In 1864, Lincoln acknowledged this reality: "I claim not to have controlled events, but confess plainly that events have controlled me. Now, at the end of three years struggle the nation's condition is not what either party, or any man devised, or expected. God alone can claim it." These words lead us to reconsider the question—was Lincoln a Christian? Bearing in mind the amorphous quality of Protestantism and recalling Lincoln's exemplary, Christian-like ethical behavior, we are still confounded by the enigmatic nature of Lincoln's religion. This may suggest that his religion cannot be confined within definitive parameters. Although the civil war saw the religious skeptic of Springfield come to terms with a God working through history, he never quite fit the mold of the "church-going Christian." Was Lincoln a Christian? The enigma remains.

HISTORIOGRAPHY ON
LINCOLN AND RELIGION

Richard W. Etulain

In the nearly sixteen thousand books written about Abraham Lincoln, a handful of subjects have captured major attention. Lincoln as a politician active in party politics has undoubtedly gained the most space, but studies of Lincoln and race have become particularly popular since the 1960s. In another area, examinations of Lincoln's attitudes about slavery and his role in the Emancipation Proclamation overlap his political activities and his statements about race.

Historians and biographers have also focused on the subject of Abraham Lincoln and religion. Indeed, the increasing interest in this topic in the past half century makes it one of the half dozen or so most emphasized Lincoln subjects. The interpretations of Lincoln and religion divide into three rather well defined periods. In the first half century after Lincoln's death, stories of Lincoln as a devout Christian or as a rational nonbeliever competed for dominance. In the next fifty years, up to the mid-1960s, interest in Lincoln as a religious thinker or participant plummeted, nearly disappearing from the historiographical scene. But in the two generations and more since the 1960s, Lincoln and religion has returned as a popular subject among Lincoln scholars and biographers. In fact, in the last twenty years, Lincoln's religious ideas and their influences on his political choices have become a major subject of discussion. In the foregoing pages, Ferenc M. Szasz illustrates well this recent trend in linking Lincoln's religious ideas to his political decisions. This essay attempts, very briefly, to trace these historiographical currents. Books and essays mentioned here in abbreviated form are fully cited in the volume's appended bibliography.

By the early years of the twentieth century, two conflicting views of Abraham Lincoln and religion were in place. They had evolved from early interpretations appearing soon after Lincoln's assassination in April 1865. At one end of the spectrum were writers like Josiah Holland, whose best-selling *Life of Abraham Lincoln* (1866) portrayed the sixteenth president as "eminently a Christian." A strongly committed Christian himself, Holland had little trouble portraying Lincoln as a devoutly religious man who knew the Bible and became more faithful as a horrendous war pressed in on him. Isaac N. Arnold, a long-time congressman from Illinois and Lincoln's friend, turned the president into a virtual saint in a summing-up chapter (674–90) in his *The History of Abraham Lincoln and the Overthrow of Slavery* (1866). In similar fashion, in his book *The Life and Public Services of Abraham Lincoln* (1865), newspaperman Henry J. Raymond, drawing on the remembrances of portrait artist "Frank" Carpenter, asserted of Lincoln "a sincerer Christian I believe never lived," although he admitted Lincoln "could scarcely be called a *religious* man, in the common acceptation of the term" (731).

At the other end of the spectrum, far from those who portrayed Lincoln as an orthodox Christian, was William Herndon, Lincoln's third law partner. Convinced that Holland and others portraying Lincoln as a man of faith were producing "all bosh," Herndon asserted that reason, not blind devotion, guided Lincoln. Herndon never completed his own full biography of his law partner, but he gave public lecturers that included descriptions of Lincoln as a skeptic or nonbeliever. Herndon also funneled off his research, particularly his invaluable interviews and oral histories, to other writers who wrote books about Lincoln as a religious doubter. The earliest of these book-length studies was *The Life of Abraham Lincoln* (1872), said to be authored by Ward H. Lamon, Lincoln's acquaintance and bodyguard, but actually ghostwritten by Chauncey F. Black. The volume included little about religion but did state that "perhaps no phase of his [Lincoln's] character has been more persistently misrepresented and variously misunderstood, than this of his religious belief" (486). Lamon and Black incorporated quotes from several of Lincoln's intimate acquaintances to substantiate their view that Lincoln was an unorthodox Christian, primarily a freethinker who did not accept the divinity of Christ or the inspiration of the Bible. When Herndon finally found a willing collaborator in Jesse W. Weik, they coauthored *Herndon's Lincoln: The True Story of a Great Life* (1889) in three volumes. The authors were straightforward in their conclusions: "Lincoln was enthusiastic in his infidelity" (Wilson and Davis, *Herndon's Lincoln*, 266). Herndon stubbornly held to this conclusion that Lincoln was in no wise a believing Christian.

Mary Lincoln unwittingly added fuel to Herndon's fire—and to those who thought Lincoln not a religious person. She told an interviewer that "Lincoln had no hope & no faith in the usual acceptation of those words: he never joined a Church . . . he was not a technical Christian" (Wilson and Davis, *Herndon's Informants*, 360).

Revealingly, the most extensive early biography of Lincoln, John G. Nicolay and John Hay's *Abraham Lincoln: A History* (10 vols., 1886–90), contains very little on Lincoln's religious ideas. In this multivolume history, political discussions are extensive, and even lengthier are the treatments of Civil War battles and administrative decisions. Nicolay and Hay provide thorough information on the public Lincoln but little on the private president.

If biographers and historians early on seemed reluctant to do much with Lincoln and religion, one minister-turned-author was much less hesitant. Indeed, William E. Barton's thorough study, *The Soul of Abraham Lincoln* (1920), became an early benchmark in examinations of Lincoln's religious journey. An active minister who later retired to devote himself full-time to his Lincoln studies, Barton produced an extensive, balanced, and skeptically nuanced examination of Lincoln's religious views. He argued against what he considered the excessive and sometimes unfounded views of Herndon but also questioned the conclusions of those who wanted an entirely orthodox Lincoln. Some critics think Barton was arrogant, too convinced of his own rightness, but, before most others, he urged readers to consider the evolutionary nature of Lincoln's religious pilgrimage, a view increasingly popular among most Lincoln specialists.

In the next fifty years, the first Lincoln scholars came on the scene, and some of the all-time best-selling books on Lincoln appeared. Yet neither the scholars nor the best sellers did much with Lincoln and religion. But, interestingly, a theologian did provide a pioneering study of the subject.

The first widely recognized Lincoln scholar was James G. Randall of the University of Illinois. Toward the end of his career, Randall finished three volumes and part of the fourth on Lincoln titled *Lincoln the President* (1945–55), which his student Richard Current completed in 1991. Surprisingly little on Lincoln and religion appears in these thoroughly researched and analytically polished volumes. Randall and Current write that Lincoln's fatalism—his conclusions that God decided what happened, that man sometimes became the agent of an all-powerful God's purposes, and that the Civil War illustrated a God-ordained world—hardened in the presidential years. Lincoln could make some space for human actions within this predestined world but not much. In a final concluding chapter titled "God's Man" (4:365–79), probably written by Current but based on Randall's notes, the authors conclude, "Since Lincoln's death, more words have been wasted on the question of his [Lincoln's] religion than on any other aspect of his life" (372). The authors assert that preachers transformed Lincoln into a martyred Christian saint, and others also claimed too much. Still, he "was a man of more intense religiosity than any other President the United States has ever had" (375).

The Randall volumes became widely accepted as *the* scholarly books on Lincoln after their publication in the 1940s and 1950s, but it was the six volumes of poet Carl Sandburg that became the best sellers. General readers snapped them up by the hundreds of thousands.

Sandburg made his first mark as a Lincoln specialist with the appearance of the two-volume *Abraham Lincoln: The Prairie Years* (1926). Here, Sandburg's treatment of Lincoln's religious ideas is brief, scattered, and provocative. The author's anecdotal approach leans away from thesis or conclusion, leaving his strings of stories rather disjointed. But taken together, these tales portray a young man and mature adult as both a God-seeker and a doubter. As is true of most of what Sandburg produced about Lincoln, the strength of this account is the plethora of lively, interest-whetting anecdotes about a folk Lincoln.

Sandburg's four-volume *Abraham Lincoln: The War Years* (1939), published more than a dozen years later, followed the format of his earlier Lincoln books but also added more information on Lincoln's religious ideas. Sandburg refers to Lincoln's thoughts about God's will and its workings in the world, Lincoln's decision to establish Thanksgiving, and statements by Secretary of State William Seward and Secretary of War Edwin Stanton about Lincoln's thoughts on religion. In the only extended discussion of Lincoln's use of laughter and his religious ideas (3:367–82), Sandburg employs anecdotal, humorous, descriptive, and unanalytical comments but does not speak of the religious references in the Second Inaugural Address. Sandburg does provide something of a conclusion on the general subject, however: "What Lincoln had of mystic faith and inner outlook was of hidden and slowly incessant growth" (3:381).

In 1952, Benjamin P. Thomas published what was touted as the best one-volume biography of Lincoln during the next two generations. *Abraham Lincoln: A Biography* deserved the high acclaim. It was smoothly written, lively, and interesting, and it was the first one-volume biography to have access to the newly opened Robert Todd Lincoln Papers at the Library of Congress. (Nicolay and Hay used the papers before Lincoln's son Robert deposited and sealed them until 1947.) Thomas was much less inclined to accept the revisionist or "Blundering Generation" thesis of James G. Randall. Instead, Thomas's Lincoln was a great, good man who led a country deceptively well in troublesome times. Still, Thomas was little interested in race or religion; neither of these topics receive extended coverage in his well-received account.

If historians and biographers seemed little intrigued with Lincoln's religious ideas between 1920 and the 1960s, theologian William J. Wolf stepped into the gap with his path-breaking book *The Almost Chosen People: A Study of the Religion of Abraham Lincoln* (1959). More than a half century after its publication, Wolf's book remains, some think, the best study of this important topic. Wolf, a seminary professor with a doctorate in theology, was a diligent researcher in pertinent primary and secondary sources and critically examined the stories about Lincoln's faith, or lack thereof. Most important, as he moved chronologically through Lincoln's pre-presidential and White House years, Wolf connected Lincoln's religious beliefs to specific actions. For example, he includes an illuminating discussion of how

Lincoln's religious ideas were at the center of his formulation and announcement of the Emancipation Proclamation. In Wolf's linkages between Lincoln's religious faith and notable events of his life, he moves beyond what earlier as well as twentieth-century historians, biographers, and Lincoln specialists had done, foreshadowing an approach to Lincoln and religion increasingly widespread in the past generation or two. Quaker philosopher and theologian Elton Trueblood added markedly to Wolf's important book in his own volume, *Abraham Lincoln: Theologian of American Anguish* (1973). Trueblood expands on Lincoln's anguish in trying to find man's role in serving God's purposes and how he, as president, could follow God's will in freeing slaves and upholding the Union.

Two shifts in historical writing in the 1970s and 1980s markedly influenced studies of Lincoln and religion. First, as historians bundled more closely with social scientists, particularly cultural anthropologists and sociologists interested in the "culture concept," they exhibited an enlarging interest in religion. The new interests were not so much in religion as a theological system but as a major ingredient of "culture," a holistic view of the beliefs and values of a people. In the second half of the 1970s, with the evangelical Jimmy Carter in the White House, whom many historians had voted for, their writings revealed much greater interest in the coverage of diverse religious cultures in the United States. Second, writing about American religion became more acceptable as historians tried to investigate the full spectrum of American sociocultural history. One could now study evangelicals, their ideas, and their actions, for example, without being considered off-track professionally. Following that new trend was another that emphasized what William Wolf had done earlier: providing strong and revealing links between one's religious persuasions and actions deriving from those religious motivations.

The writings of three of Lincoln's recent biographers clearly illustrate the expanding interest in Lincoln and religion. The first was Allen Guelzo's pathbreaking intellectual biography *Abraham Lincoln: Redeemer President* (1999). Already a widely published authority on New England minister Jonathan Edwards and American religion, Guelzo put his large understanding of the labyrinthine intricacies of Calvinism to work in discussing the religious journey of Lincoln. In his sophisticated biography, Guelzo delineates the complexities of Calvinist doctrine, especially its concepts of predestination and an all-powerful God, and the shaping power of these ideas on his subject's thoughts and actions. Lincoln may have rejected the Hardshell Baptist churches of his parents, Guelzo notes, but the Calvinistic teachings of those churches seeped into his own thinking, as his "Meditation on the Divine Will" and the Second Inaugural clearly showed. More than previous biographers, Guelzo portrays Lincoln as a reader, thinker, and intellectual; and on the canvas of Lincoln's inward sky, Guelzo paints in revealing hues Lincoln's transitions as a religious thinker from youthful skepticism to increasing acceptance of much Christian thinking—without becoming a "true believer." Guelzo also brings together several of his other provocative essays, including the notable piece "Abraham Lincoln and the Doctrine of Necessity" (27–48), in his *Abraham Lincoln as a Man of Ideas* (2009).

Another superb work for placing Lincoln in American religious contexts of his time is a biography by British scholar Richard J. Carwardine. *Lincoln* (2003; reprinted in the United States as *Lincoln: A Life of Purpose and Power*, 2006) builds on the author's earlier—and very perceptive—studies of nineteenth-century American religion. In addition, as Carwardine told an interviewer, he could not understand Lincoln's uses of power without comprehending the president's religious and moral predilections. Lincoln also understood and used the power of northern Protestant groups to lead the Union during the Civil War. Like Guelzo and biographer Ronald C. White, Carwardine links religion and politics to illuminate Lincoln's character and actions. Carwardine provides a succinct, first-rate examination of some of these topics in his valuable essay "Lincoln's Religion."

Ronald C. White rivals Guelzo and Carwardine in his thorough treatment of Lincoln's religious views and their influences on his decisions. In White's superbly written life story *A. Lincoln: A Biography* (2009), he devotes nearly fifty pages to Lincoln's stuttering but rather steady steps toward acceptance of facets of Christianity. White's discussions of Presbyterian ministers James Smith (in Springfield) and Phineas D. Gurley (in Washington, D.C.) are particularly illuminating. Moreover, the author's conclusion fits well with those of many other recent scholars: "Lincoln underwent a religious odyssey that deepened as he aged, inquiring about everlasting truths until his last day" (676).

Not all recent biographers have viewed Lincoln's religious journey in the same light, however. Stephen B. Oates in his *With Malice toward None: The Life of Abraham Lincoln* (1977) and David Herbert Donald in his *Lincoln* (1995)—both of which were considered outstanding one-volume biographies at their publication—show scant interest in Lincoln's religious views. Oates's work, illustrating the heavy emphasis of contemporary historians on politics and changing views on slavery, pays little attention to religion. Donald shows more interest in Lincoln's religious ideas, discussing Lincoln's Bible reading, his letters expressing belief in God, and his invoking of Providence. But those discussions are much less thorough and probing than Donald's extensive comments on Lincoln and politics and on Lincoln and race. And, surprisingly, Michael Burlingame, so painstakingly complete on numerous subjects in his huge two-volume *Abraham Lincoln: A Life* (2008), does little with Lincoln's religious pilgrimage. He briefly discusses Lincoln religious ideas in the pre-1861 years but says very little about the subject after Lincoln entered the presidency.

Other historians and political scientists were finding new ways to understand religious influences on Lincoln. In his book *Abraham Lincoln's Political Faith* (2003), political theorist Joseph R. Fornieri writes of Lincoln's "Biblical Republicanism" and demonstrates how Lincoln's adept uses of biblical and other religious wisdom and guidance helped the president to deal with vexing political issues. Historian Stewart Winger, in his *Lincoln, Religion, and Romantic Cultural Politics* (2002), discusses how Whig stances on "positive moral government" shaped Lincoln's thinking. The Whig-evangelical alliance—encompassing competing ideologies of determinism and individual responsibility—appears in Lincoln's thinking in the Second Inaugural, Winger says. Still another historian, Lucas E. Morel in his essay "Lincoln, God, and Freedom: A Promise Fulfilled," demonstrates how Lincoln's "view of the will of God" led to emancipation. If God gave the Union a victory in 1862, Lincoln told his cabinet in July of that year, he would view it as a sign of God's will and move ahead with the Emancipation Proclamation. In these books and essays, writers coined new terms to deal with the marriage of politics and religion in Lincoln's thinking and actions: Lincoln as civil theologian, as a political theologian, as an exemplar of civil or political religion. Perhaps David Hein puts it most succinctly in his essay "Lincoln's Theology and Political Ethics": "Lincoln's ethics were theocentric, God-centered; . . . his political ethics are incapable of being grasped apart from his theology."

Scholars in religion and literature were providing still other illuminating insights about Lincoln's religious views and their influences on his decisions. In his valuable volume *America's God: From Jonathan Edwards to Abraham Lincoln* (2002), Mark Noll, one of the country's leading historians of religion, illuminates Lincoln's religiosity through a close examination of the Second Inaugural. He concludes that Lincoln's "magnanimity and his moral evenhandedness were generally religious, and his view of providence was distinctively theological. More than any other feature of this address, Lincoln's conceptions of God's rule over the world set him apart from the recognized theologians of his day" (427). Focusing on the same document in his book *Upon the Altar of the Nation: A Moral History of the American Civil War* (2006), Harry Stout, another historian of American religion, argues that Lincoln "was becoming steadily more spiritual, although without compromising his unshaken resolve." Even though many northern clergy were convinced that God was on their side in the fratricidal war, "Lincoln, almost alone, was not convinced. He too had a growing sense of Providence, but without the self-righteous evangelical piety that went along with so much patriotism in the North and South" (145).

Literature scholar A. E. Elmore furnishes still another way to approach Lincoln and religion in his monographic work *Lincoln's Gettysburg Address: Echoes of the Bible and Book of Common Prayer* (2009). Clearly Elmore has nineteenth-century, twentieth-century, and twenty-first-century meanings in mind as he closely examines every word of Lincoln's classic address. He wants post-2000 readers to understand fully how Lincoln, borrowing ideas from two wide-ly read books—the King James Bible and the Book of Common Prayer—spoke for his times. The author accepts Lincoln's personal, white, self-centered human qualities but brings them alongside the president's humanitarian, forward-looking, and compassionate views, especially those on ending slavery, avoiding retribution, and call-ing for increasing equality for blacks. The volume's chief purpose, Elmore asserts, is to go "beyond literary analysis to trace the moral and political meanings that Abraham Lincoln clearly intended to convey in his greatest speech" (7).

In 1998, Lincoln scholar Ronald White concluded that "major Lincoln biographers of the past half-century [had] treated Lincoln's religious views quite sparingly" and that "academic historians have not wasted many words on Lincoln's religion" ("Lincoln's Sermon on the Mount," 223, 224). That assertion, quite true fifteen years ago, no longer holds. Biographers Allen Guelzo, Richard Carwardine, and White himself have published biographies of Lincoln that clearly and appealingly depict the close and influential links between Lin-coln's religious ideas and his presidential decisions. Historians such as Joseph Fornieri, Stewart Winger, and Lucas Morel have created a new vocabulary in treating connections between Lincoln's religios-ity and his political ideas. Meanwhile, scholars of American religion and literature, such as Mark Noll, Harry Stout, and A. E. Elmore, have also posited close ties between Lincoln, religion, and his politi-cal and administrative decisions. Nearly all these authorities agree, too, that Lincoln's religious journey was certainly evolving, from the earlier skepticism to a stance that more closely resembled traditional Christian views.

Obviously, a swift, manifest historiographical shift has taken place. A nearly unanimous consensus seems evident: Lincoln's re-ligious ideas were not only central to his personal beliefs but also frequently and distinctly shaped his political and moral decisions. Have we seen the last word on Lincoln and religion? Of course not. That is as likely as a moratorium on all new Lincoln books. But view-ing Lincoln's spiritual journey as a series of sometimes faltering but usually steady steps from the earlier skepticism to the later view of a God-ordained universe seems acceptable to—indeed, widespread among—many leading Lincoln specialists. The promoters of an infidel, unbelieving Lincoln are gone.

Ferenc Morton Szasz's succinct overview in this volume illustrates these recent trends in the study of Lincoln and religion. As Szasz deftly shows, Lincoln's early years exposed him to what historians of American religion later termed frontier revivalism and fundamentalism. Lincoln did not follow those teachings, however; he moved away from these rather rigid Calvinistic doctrines in his early years in New Salem and Springfield. But the deaths of sons Eddie and Willie, and Lincoln's grief following those deaths, as well as his positive connections with Presbyterian pastors James Smith and Phineas D. Gurley, softened Lincoln's critical attitude toward religious teachings. The horrendous responsibilities of the four-year war and the unrelenting pressures of presidential leadership brought Lincoln even closer to traditional Christianity, reawakening him especially to the enigmatic role of God's will in human history. These moves toward faith influenced Lincoln's attitudes and decisions. As Szasz clearly demonstrates, Lincoln's decision to issue the Emancipation Proclamation, his dealings with several religious groups, his correspondence with numerous supporters and critics, and his Second Inaugural were revealing epiphanies of his journey toward a deeper faith.

LINCOLN ON RELIGION: QUOTATIONS
Compiled by Sara Gabbard

Abraham Lincoln frequently referred to God in both public speeches and private letters. Included below are some examples that are well known and some that are not. All material is taken from *The Collected Works of Abraham Lincoln*, ed. Roy P. Basler, 9 vols. (New Brunswick, NJ: Rutgers UP, 1953–55).

Official Presidential Proclamations, Addresses, and Letters

First Inaugural Address (March 4, 1861)

If the Almighty Ruler of nations, with his eternal truth and justice, be on your side of the North, or on yours of the South, that truth, and that justice, will surely prevail, by the judgment of this great tribunal, the American people. . . . Intelligence, patriotism, Christianity, and a firm reliance on Him, who has never yet forsaken this favored land, are still competent to adjust, in the best way, all our present difficulty.

Message to Congress in Special Session (July 4, 1861)

And having thus chosen our course, without guile, and with pure purpose, let us renew our trust in God, and go forward without fear, and with manly hearts.

Proclamation of a National Fast Day (August 12, 1861)

Whereas a joint Committee of both Houses of Congress has waited on the President of the United States, and requested him to "recommend a day of public humiliation, prayer and fasting, to be observed by the people of the United States with religious solemnity, and the offering of fervent supplications to Almighty God for the safety and welfare of these States, His blessings on their arms, and a speedy restoration of peace:"—

And whereas it is fit and becoming in all people, at all times, to acknowledge and revere the Supreme Government of God; to bow in humble submission to his chastisements; to confess and deplore their sins and transgressions in the full conviction that the fear of the Lord is the beginning of wisdom; and to pray, with all fervency and contrition, for the pardon of their past offenses, and for a blessing upon their present and prospective action:

And whereas, when our own beloved Country, once, by the blessing of God, united, prosperous and happy, is now afflicted with faction and civil war, it is peculiarly fit for us to recognize the hand of God in this terrible visitation, and in sorrowful remembrance of our own faults and crimes as a nation and as individuals, to humble ourselves before Him, and to pray for His mercy—to pray that we may be spared further punishment, though most justly deserved; that our arms may be blessed and made effectual for the re-establishment of law, order and peace, throughout the wide extent of our country; and that the inestimable boon of civil and religious liberty, earned under His guidance and blessing, by the labors and sufferings of our fathers, may be restored in all its original excellence:—

Therefore, I, Abraham Lincoln, President of the United States, do appoint the last Thursday in September next, as a day of humiliation, prayer and fasting for all the people of the nation. And I do earnestly recommend to all the People, and especially to all ministers and teachers of religion of all denominations, and to all heads of families, to observe and keep that day according to their several creeds and modes of worship, in all humility and with all religious solemnity, to the end that the united prayer of the nation may ascend to the Throne of Grace and bring down plentiful blessings upon our Country.

Proclamation of Thanksgiving for Victories (April 10, 1862)

It has pleased Almighty God to vouchsafe signal victories to the land and naval forces engaged in suppressing an internal rebellion, and at the same time to avert from our country the dangers of foreign intervention and invasion.

It is therefore recommended to the People of the United States that, at their next weekly assemblages in their accustomed places of public worship which shall occur after notice of this proclamation shall have been received, they especially acknowledge and render thanks to our Heavenly Father for these inestimable blessings; that they then and there implore spiritual consolations in behalf of all who have been brought into affliction by the casualties and calamities of sedition and civil war, and that they reverently invoke the Divine Guidance for our national counsels, to the end that they may speedily result in the restoration of peace, harmony, and unity throughout our borders, and hasten the establishment of fraternal relations among all the countries of the earth.

Emancipation Proclamation (January 1, 1863)

And upon this act, sincerely believed to be an act of justice, warranted by the Constitution, upon military necessity, I invoke the considerate judgment of mankind, and the gracious favor of Almighty God.

Annual Message to Congress (December 8, 1863; referring to treatment of "Indian Tribes")

Sound policy and our imperative duty to these wards of the government demand our anxious and constant attention to their material well-being, to their progress in the arts of civilization, and, above all, to that moral training which, under the blessing of Divine Providence, will confer upon them the elevated and sanctifying influences, the hopes and consolation of the Christian faith.

Reply to Loyal Colored People of Baltimore upon Presentation of a Bible (September 7, 1864)

In regard to this Great Book, I have but to say, it is the best gift God has given to man.

All the good the Saviour gave to the world was communicated through this book. But for it we could not know right from wrong. All things most desirable for man's welfare, here and hereafter, are to be found portrayed in it. To you I return my most sincere thanks for the very elegant copy of the great Book of God which you present.

Second Inaugural Address (March 4, 1865)

Both read the same Bible, and pray to the same God; and each invokes His aid against the other. It may seem strange that any men should dare to ask a just God's assistance in wringing their bread from the sweat of other men's faces; but let us judge not that we be not judged. The prayers of both could not be answered; that of neither has been answered fully. The Almighty has His own purposes. "Woe unto the world because of offences! for it must needs be that offences come; but woe to that man by whom the offence cometh!" If we shall suppose that American Slavery is one of those offences which, in the providence of God, must needs come, but which, having continued through His appointed time, He now wills to remove, and that He gives to both North and South, this terrible war, as the woe due to those by whom the offence came, shall we discern therein any departure from those divine attributes which the believers in a Living God always ascribe to Him? Fondly do we hope—fervently do we pray—that this mighty scourge of war may speedily pass away. Yet, if God wills that it continue, until all the wealth piled by the bond-man's two hundred and fifty years of unrequited toil shall be sunk, and until every drop of blood drawn with the lash, shall be paid by another drawn with the sword, as was said three thousand years ago, so still it must be said "the judgments of the Lord, are true and righteous altogether."

Personal Letters

Letter to John D. Johnston (January 12, 1851)

When Lincoln was told that his father was gravely ill, he replied to Johnston that he would provide for his father and stepmother's "want of any comfort either in health or sickness," but he could not leave home because Mary was "sick a-bed." He then wrote:

I sincerely hope Father may yet recover his health; but at all events tell him to remember to call upon, and confide in, our great, and good, and merciful Maker; who will not turn away from him in any extremity. He notes the fall of a sparrow, and numbers the hairs of our heads; and He will not forget the dying man, who puts his trust in Him. Say to him that if we could meet now, it is doubtful whether it would not be more painful than pleasant; but that if it be his lot to go now, he will soon have a joyous [meeting] with many loved ones gone before; and where [the rest] of us, through the help of God, hope ere-long [to join] them.

To Queen Victoria (February 1, 1862; condolences on the death of "His Royal Highness the late Prince Consort, Prince Albert, of Saxe Coburg")

This condolence may not be altogether ineffectual, since we are sure it emanates from only virtuous motives and natural affection. I do not dwell upon it, however, because I know that the Divine hand that has wounded, is the only one that can heal: And so, commending Your Majesty and the Prince Royal, the Heir Apparent, and all your afflicted family to the tender mercies of God, I remain

Your Good Friend, Abraham Lincoln

Reply to Eliza P. Gurney (October 26, 1862)

I am glad of this interview, and glad to know that I have your sympathy and prayers. We are indeed going through a great trial—a fiery trial. In the very responsible position in which I happen to be placed, being a humble instrument in the hands of our Heavenly Father, as I am, and as we all are, to work out his great purposes, I have desired that all my works and acts may be according to his will, and that it might be so, I have sought his aid—but if after endeavoring to do my best in the light which he affords me, I find my efforts fail, I must believe that for some purpose unknown to me, He wills it otherwise. If I had had my way, this war would never have been commenced; If I had been allowed my way this war would have been ended before this, but we find it still continues; and we must believe that He permits it for some wise purpose of his own, mysterious and unknown to us; and though with our limited understandings we may not be able to comprehend it, yet we cannot but believe, that he who made the world still governs it.

Letter to Mrs. Lydia Bixby (November 21, 1864)

Dear Madam,—I have been shown in the files of the War Department a statement of the Adjutant General of Massachusetts, that you are the mother of five sons who have died gloriously of the field of battle.

I feel how weak and fruitless must be any words of mine which should attempt to beguile you from the grief of a loss so overwhelming. But I cannot refrain from tendering to you the consolation that may be found in the thanks of the Republic they died to save.

I pray that our Heavenly Father may assuage the anguish of your bereavement, and leave you only the cherished memory of the loved and lost, and the solemn pride that must be yours, to have laid so costly a sacrifice upon the altar of Freedom.

Miscellaneous

Address to Springfield Washington Temperance Society (February 22, 1842)

By the Washingtonians, this system of consigning the habitual drunkard to hopeless ruin, is repudiated. *They* adopt a more enlarged philanthropy. *They* go for present as well as future good. *They* labor for all *now* living, as well as all *hereafter* to live. *They* teach *hope* to all—*despair* to none. As applying to *their* cause, *they* deny the doctrine of unpardonable sin. As in Christianity it is taught, so in this *they* teach, that "While the lamp holds out to burn, / The vilest sinner may return."

Fragment: Niagara Falls (ca. September 25–30, 1848)

Niagara-Falls! By what mysterious power is it that millions and millions, are drawn from all parts of the world, to gaze upon Niagara Falls? . . . It calls up the indefinite past. When Columbus first sought this continent—when Christ suffered on the cross—when Moses led Israel through the Red-Sea—nay, even, when Adam first came from the hand of his Maker—then as now, Niagara was roaring here.

Eulogy on Henry Clay (July 6, 1852)

But Henry Clay is dead. His long and eventful life is closed. Our country is prosperous and powerful; but could it have been quite all it has been, and is, and is to be, without Henry Clay? Such a man the times have demanded, and such, in the providence of God was given us. But he is gone. Let us strive to deserve, as far as mortals may, the continued care of Divine Providence, trusting that, in future national emergencies, He will not fail to provide us the instruments of safety and security.

Speech at Chicago, Illinois (July 10, 1858)

My friend has said to me that I am a poor hand to quote Scripture. I will try it again, however. It is said in one of the admonitions of the Lord, "As your Father in Heaven is perfect, be ye also perfect." The Savior, I suppose, did not expect that any human creature could be perfect as the Father in Heaven; but He said, "As your Father in Heaven is perfect, be ye also perfect." He set that up as a standard, and he who did most towards reaching that standard, attained the highest degree of moral perfection. So I say in relation to the principle that all men are created equal, let it be as nearly reached as we can. If we cannot give freedom to every creature, let us do nothing that will impose slavery upon any other creature.

Speech at Lewiston, Illinois (August 17, 1858; speaking on the Declaration of Independence)

These communities, by their representatives in old Independence Hall, said to the whole world of men: "We hold these truths to be self evident: that all men are created equal; that they are endowed by their Creator with certain unalienable rights; that among these are life, liberty and the pursuit of happiness." This was their majestic interpretation of the economy of the Universe. This was their lofty, and wise, and noble understanding of the justice of the Creator to His creatures. Yes, gentlemen, to *all* His creatures, to the whole great family of man. . . . Wise statesmen as they were, they knew the tendency of prosperity to breed tyrants, and so they established these great self-evident truths, that when in the distant future some man, some faction, some interest, should set up the doctrine that none but rich men, or none but white men, were entitled to life, liberty and the pursuit of happiness, their posterity might look up again to the Declaration of Independence and take courage to renew the battle which their fathers began—so that truth, and justice, and mercy, and all the humane and Christian virtues might not be extinguished from the land; so that no man would hereafter dare to limit and circumscribe the great principles on which the temple of liberty was being built.

Address at Cooper Institute, New York City (February 27, 1860)

Let us be diverted by none of those sophistical contrivances wherewith we are so industriously plied and belabored—contrivances such as groping for some middle ground between the right and the wrong, vain as the search for a man who should be neither a living man nor a dead man—such as a policy of "don't care" on a question about which all true men do care—such as Union appeals beseeching true Union men to yield to Disunionists, reversing the divine rule, and calling, not the sinners, but the righteous to repentance . . .

BIBLIOGRAPHY

Angle, Paul M. *"Here I have lived": A History of Lincoln's Springfield, 1821–1865.* 1935. Chicago: Abraham Lincoln Book Shop, 1971.

Armstrong, Karen. "Charter for Compassion: At One with Our Ignorance." *Guardian Weekly* Nov. 20, 2009.

Arnold, Isaac N. *The History of Abraham Lincoln and the Overthrow of Slavery.* Chicago: Clarke & Co., 1866.

Arrington, Leonard J. *Brigham Young: American Moses.* New York: Knopf, 1985.

The Assassination of Abraham Lincoln: A Tribute of the Nations. Old Saybrook, CT: Konecky and Konecky, 2009.

Barbee, David Rankin. "President Lincoln and Doctor Gurley." *Abraham Lincoln Quarterly* 5 (Mar. 1948): 3–24.

Barton, William Eleazar. *The Soul of Abraham Lincoln.* 1920. Urbana: U of Illinois P, 2005.

Bennett, Lerone, Jr. *Forced into Glory: Lincoln's White Dream.* Chicago: Johnson, 2000.

Blair, William A., and Karen Fisher Younger, eds. *Lincoln's Proclamation: Emancipation Reconsidered.* Chapel Hill: U of North Carolina P, 2009.

Bobrick, Benson. *Wide and the Waters: The Story of the English Bible and the Revolution It Inspired.* New York: Penguin, 2002.

Boles, John B. *Religion in Antebellum Kentucky.* 1976. Lexington: U of Kentucky P, 1995.

Boritt, Gabor S. *Lincoln and the Economics of the American Dream.* Urbana: U of Illinois P, 1994.

Braden, Waldo, ed. *Building the Myth: Selected Speeches Memorializing Abraham Lincoln.* Urbana: U of Illinois P, 1990.

Bray, Robert. *Peter Cartwright, Legendary Frontier Preacher.* Urbana: U of Illinois P, 2005.

Brooks, Noah. *The Character and Religion of Abraham Lincoln: A Letter of Noah Brooks, May 10, 1865.* Champlain, NY: privately printed, 1919.

———. "Reflections of Abraham Lincoln." *Harper's New Monthly Magazine* July 1865: 222–30.

Burlingame, Michael. *Abraham Lincoln: A Life.* 2 vols. Baltimore: Johns Hopkins UP, 2008.

———, ed. *At Lincoln's Side: John Hay's Civil War Correspondence and Selected Writings.* Carbondale: Southern Illinois UP, 2000.

Burton, Orville Vernon. *The Age of Lincoln.* New York: Hill and Wang, 2007. An excellent contextualization of Lincoln, including his religion.

Cagle, Daryl, and Brian Fairrington, eds. *The Best Political Cartoons of the Year 2009*. Indianapolis: Que Publishing, 2009.

Carpenter, F. B. *The Inner Life of Abraham Lincoln: Six Months at the White House*. New York: Hurd and Houghton, 1869.

Cartwright, Peter. *Autobiography of Peter Cartwright, the Backwoods Preacher*. 1856. Nashville: Abingdon, 1956.

Carwardine, Richard J. *Lincoln: A Life of Purpose and Power*. New York: Knopf, 2006.

———. "Lincoln's Religion." *History Now* 18 (Dec. 2008). www.historynow. org. Dec. 17, 2009.

Chittenden, L. E. *Recollections of President Lincoln and His Administration*. New York: Harper and Brothers, 1891.

Donald, David Herbert. *Lincoln*. New York: Simon and Schuster, 1995.

Edwards, Herbert Joseph, John Erskine Hankins, and W. H. Jeffrey. *Lincoln the Writer: The Development of His Literary Style*. Orono: UP of Maine, 1962.

Elmore, A. E. *Lincoln's Gettysburg Address: Echoes of the Bible and Book of Common Prayer*. Carbondale: Southern Illinois UP, 2009.

Emerson, Ralph W. "Abraham Lincoln." *The Selected Writings of Ralph Waldo Emerson*. Ed. Brooks Atkinson. New York: Modern Library, 1940. 917–21.

Emery, Richard L. *Abraham Lincoln and the Latter-day Saints*. Bloomington, IN: Authorhouse, 2005.

Etulain, Richard W. *Lincoln Looks West*. Carbondale: Southern Illinois UP, 2009.

Finney, Charles G. *Memoirs of Rev. Charles G. Finney, Written by Himself*. New York: Fleming H. Revell Company, 1876.

Fornieri, Joseph R. *Abraham Lincoln's Political Faith*. DeKalb: Northern Illinois UP, 2003.

Gienapp, William. *Abraham Lincoln and Civil War America: A Biography*. Oxford: Oxford UP, 2002.

Greeley, Horace. "Greeley's Estimate of Lincoln, an Address by Horace Greeley." *Century Magazine* May–Oct. 1891: 371, 798.

Guelzo, Allen C. *Abraham Lincoln as a Man of Ideas*. Carbondale: Southern Illinois UP, 2009.

———. *Abraham Lincoln: Redeemer President*. Grand Rapids, MI: Eerdmans, 1999.

Hatch, Nathan O., and Mark A. Noll, eds. *The Bible in America: Essays in Cultural History*. New York: Oxford UP, 1982.

Havlik, Robert. "Abraham Lincoln and The Rev. Dr. James Smith." *Journal of the Illinois State Historical Society* 92.3 (Autumn 1999): 396–99.

Hein, David. "Lincoln's Theology and Political Ethics." *Essays on Lincoln's Faith and Politics*. By Hans J. Morgenthau and David Hein. Ed. Kenneth W. Thompson. Lanham, MD: UP of America, 1983.

Herndon, William H., and Jesse W. Weik. *Herndon's Lincoln: The True Story of a Great Life*. 3 vols. Chicago: Belford, Clarke & Co., 1889.

Holland, Josiah. *Life of Abraham Lincoln*. Springfield, MA: Gurdon Bill, 1866.

Holmes, David L. "The Domestic Missionary Movement in the Episcopal Church in the Nineteenth Century." *Beyond the Horizon: Frontiers for Mission*. Ed. Charles R. Henery. Cincinnati: Forward Movement Publications, 1986.

Horner, Henry. *Abraham Lincoln of Illinois*. Springfield: Illinois State Historical Society, 1938.

———. *Abraham Lincoln: The American Ideal*. Chicago: n.p., 1926.

Kiling, David W. *The Bible in History: How the Texts Have Shaped the Times*. New York: Oxford UP, 2004.

Lamon, Ward Hill. *The Life of Abraham Lincoln from His Birth to His Inauguration as President*. Boston: James R. Osgood, 1872.

Lebowich, Joseph. "General Ulysses S. Grant and the Jews." *American Jewish Historical Society Publications* 17 (1909): 71–80.

"Letter from the General Synod of the Reformed Presbyterian Church in America." *Reformed Presbyterian Magazine* July 1861: 231–32.

Lewis, Lloyd. *Myths after Lincoln*. New York: Press of the Readers Club, 1941.

Lincoln, Abraham. *The Collected Works of Abraham Lincoln*. Edited by Roy P. Basler. 9 vols. New Brunswick, NJ: Rutgers UP, 1953–55.

Markens, Isaac. "Lincoln and the Jews." *Publications of the American Jewish Historical Society* 17 (1909): 109–66.

Maynard, Nettie Coburn. *Was Abraham Lincoln a Spiritualist? or, Curious Revelations from the Life of a Trance Medium*. Chicago: Progressive Thinker Publishing House, 1917.

McGrath, Alister. *In the Beginning: The Story of the King James Bible and How It Changed a Nation, a Language, and a Culture*. New York: Anchor, 2001.

Mead, Sydney E. *The Nation with the Soul of a Church*. New York: Harper and Row, 1975.

Mehlman, Michael. "'There Is a Prince and a Great Man Fallen This Day in Israel': The Response of the Rabbis in America to the Assassination of Abraham Lincoln, April–June, 1865." *Lincoln Herald* 111 (Fall 2009): 205–21.

Metzger, Bruce M., and Michael D. Coogan, eds. *The Oxford Companion to the Bible*. New York: Oxford UP, 1993.

Meyer, Jeffrey F. *Myths in Stone: Religious Dimensions of Washington, D.C.* Berkeley: U of California P, 2001.

Miller, William Lee. *Lincoln's Virtues: An Ethical Biography.* New York: Knopf, 2002. One of the most serious efforts with a focus on Lincoln's morality.

Morel, Lucas E. "Lincoln, God, and Freedom: A Promise Fulfilled." *Lincoln and Freedom: Slavery, Emancipation, and the Thirteenth Amendment.* Ed. Harold Holzer and Sara Gabbard. Carbondale: Southern Illinois UP, 2007. 48–64.

———. *Lincoln's Sacred Effort: Defining Religion's Role in American Self-Government.* Lanham, MD: Lexington, 2000. Fuller than Morel's "Lincoln, God, and Freedom."

Nicholson, Adam. *God's Secretaries: The Making of the King James Bible.* New York: HarperCollins, 2003.

Nicolay, John G., and John Hay. *Abraham Lincoln: A History.* 10 vols. New York: Century Company, 1886–90.

Noll, Mark. *America's God: From Jonathan Edwards to Abraham Lincoln.* New York: Oxford UP, 2002.

Oates, Stephen B. *With Malice Toward None: The Life of Abraham Lincoln.* New York: Harper and Row, 1977.

Obama, Barack. "What I See in Lincoln's Eyes." *Time* June 26, 2005. www.time.com. April 13, 2009.

Ostergard, Philip L. *The Inspired Wisdom of Abraham Lincoln.* Carol Stream, IL: Tyndale House, 2008.

Paine, Thomas. *The Age of Reason.* Secaucus, NJ: Citadel, 1974.

Peterson, Merrill D. *Lincoln in American Memory.* New York: Oxford, 1994. A very good book relevant to chapter 3 of this book.

Pond, Fern Nance. "New Salem's Miller and Kelso." *Lincoln Herald* 52 (Dec. 1950): 26–42.

Quarles, Benjamin. *Lincoln and the Negro.* New York: Oxford UP, 1962.

Randall, James G. *Lincoln the President.* 3 vols. New York: Dodd, Mead, 1945–55.

Randall, James G., and Richard Current. *Lincoln the President.* Vol. 4. Urbana: U of Illinois P, 1991. Completed by Richard Current after the death of James Randall.

Randall, Ruth Painter. *Mary Lincoln: Biography of a Marriage.* Boston: Little, Brown, 1953.

Raphall, Morris J. *The Bible View of Slavery. A discourse, delivered at the Jewish synagogue, "Bnai Jeshurum," New York, on the day of the national fast, Jan. 4, 1861.* Delhi: Pranava, 2008.

Raymond, Henry J. *The Life and Public Services of Abraham Lincoln.* With an afterword, "Anecdotes and Reminiscences of President Lincoln," by Frank B. Carpenter. New York: Derby and Miller, 1865.

Reed, J. R. "The Later Life and Religious Sentiments of Abraham Lincoln." *Scribner's Monthly* 6 (July 1873): 333–43.

Reed, Thomas P. *Lincoln at New Salem*. N.p.: Old Salem Lincoln League, 1927.

Sandburg, Carl. *Abraham Lincoln: The Prairie Years*. 2 vols. New York: Harcourt, Brace, 1926.

———. *Abraham Lincoln: The War Years*. 4 vols. New York: Harcourt, Brace, 1939.

Sarna, Jonathan. *When General Grant Expelled the Jews*. New York: Schocken, 2012. A recent and excellent study of the incident explored in this book.

Schurz, Carl. "Abraham Lincoln." *Atlantic Monthly* June 1891: 721–50.

Scovel, James M. "Personal Recollections of Abraham Lincoln." *Lippincott's Monthly Magazine* Aug. 1889: 244–51.

Smith, James A. *The Christian's Defense*. 2 vols. Cincinnati: J. A. James, 1843.

Smith, Joseph. *The Book of Mormon*. Nauvoo, IL: Robinson and Smith, 1840.

Speed, Joshua F. *Reminiscences of Abraham Lincoln and Notes of a Visit to California—Two Lectures*. Louisville: J. P. Morton, 1884.

Stout, Harry. *Upon the Altar of the Nation: A Moral History of the American Civil War*. New York: Viking, 2006.

Szasz, Ferenc Morton. *Abraham Lincoln and Robert Burns: Connected Lives and Legends*. Carbondale: Southern Illinois UP, 2008.

———. "The Episcopal Bishops and the Trans-Mississippi West, 1865–1918." *Anglican and Episcopal History* 69.3 (Sept. 2000): 348–70.

Thomas, Benjamin P. *Abraham Lincoln: A Biography*. New York: Knopf, 1952.

———. *Lincoln's New Salem*. Carbondale: Southern Illinois UP, 1954.

Thomas, Christopher A. *The Lincoln Memorial and American Life*. Princeton: Princeton UP, 2002.

Trueblood, Elton. *Abraham Lincoln: Theologian of American Anguish*. New York: Harper and Row, 1973.

Twain, Mark. *The Adventures of Huckleberry Finn*. New York: Random House, 1996.

Volney, C. F. *The Ruins, or Meditation on the Revolution of Empires: And the Law of Nature*. Baltimore: Black Classic, 1991.

Warren, Louis A. *Lincoln's Youth: Indiana Years, 1816–1830*. Indianapolis: Indiana History Society, 1991. The best study of which I am aware treating the Lincoln family's religion and its local contexts.

Webster, Noah. *A Compendious Dictionary of the English Language*. New York: Bounty, 1970.

Welles, Gideon. *Diary of Gideon Welles: Secretary of the Navy under Lincoln and Johnson*. 3 vols. 1901. Boston: Houghton Mifflin, 1910.

White, Ronald C. *A. Lincoln: A Biography*. New York: Random House, 2009.

———. *The Eloquent President: A Portrait of Lincoln through His Words.* New York: Random House, 2005.

———. "Lincoln's Sermon on the Mount: The Second Inaugural." *Religion and the American Civil War.* Ed. Randall M. Miller, Harry S. Stout, and Charles Reagan Wilson. New York: Oxford UP, 1998. 208–25.

Wills, Garry. *Lincoln at Gettysburg: The Words That Remade America.* New York: Simon and Schuster, 1992.

Wilson, Douglas L. *Lincoln's Sword: The Presidency and the Power of the Words.* New York: Random House, 2006.

Wilson, Douglas L., and Rodney O. Davis, eds. *Herndon's Informants: Letters, Interviews and Statements about Abraham Lincoln.* Urbana: U of Illinois P, 1998.

———, eds. *Herndon's Lincoln.* Urbana: U of Illinois P, 2006.

Winger, Stewart. *Lincoln, Religion, and Romantic Cultural Politics.* DeKalb: Northern Illinois UP, 2002.

Wolf, William J. *The Almost Chosen People: A Study of the Religion of Abraham Lincoln.* Garden City, NY: Doubleday, 1959.

INDEX

Ferenc Morton Szasz, Regents Professor of History, taught at the University of New Mexico for over four decades. Widely known for his teaching and publications in American social and intellectual history, he focused on the history of American religion, World War II, and the atomic age. His best-known works include *The Day the Sun Rose Twice, Religion in the Modern American West*, and *Abraham Lincoln and Robert Burns: Connected Lives and Legends* (the last published by Southern Illinois University Press).

Margaret Connell Szasz, also Regents Professor of History, has taught at the University of New Mexico for several decades. Although her teaching and publishing focus on Native American history and modern Celtic history, including her books *Education and the American Indian: The Road to Self-Determination* and *Scottish Highlanders and Native Americans: Indigenous Education in the Eighteenth-Century Atlantic World*, she and Ferenc collaborated on a few works, including an essay, "Religion and Spirituality," that appeared in the *Oxford History of the American West*.

CONCISE
LINCOLN
LIBRARY

This series of concise books fills a need for short studies of the life, times, and legacy of President Abraham Lincoln. Each book gives readers the opportunity to quickly achieve basic knowledge of a Lincoln-related topic. These books bring fresh perspectives to well-known topics, investigate previously overlooked subjects, and explore in greater depth topics that have not yet received book-length treatment. For a complete list of current and forthcoming titles, see www.conciselincolnlibrary.com.

Other Books in the Concise Lincoln Library

*Abraham Lincoln and
Horace Greeley*
Gregory A. Borchard

Lincoln and the Civil War
Michael Burlingame

Lincoln and the Constitution
Brian R. Dirck

Lincoln and the Election of 1860
Michael S. Green

Lincoln and the Union Governors
William C. Harris

*Lincoln's Campaign
Biographies*
Thomas A. Horrocks

Lincoln and Reconstruction
John C. Rodrigue

Lincoln and Medicine
Glenna R. Schroeder-Lein

*Lincoln and the U.S.
Colored Troops*
John David Smith

Lincoln and Race
Richard Striner

Lincoln as Hero
Frank J. Williams

*Abraham and
Mary Lincoln*
Kenneth J. Winkle